The Student Newspaper

AMERICAN COUNCIL ON EDUCATION

83

The Student Newspaper

The Commission

Appointed by President,
University of California,
Charles J. Hitch

NORMAN E. ISAACS, *Chairman*
Vice-president and Executive Editor,
Courier-Journal and *Louisville-Times;*
President, American Society of
Newspaper Editors

WILLIAM B. ARTHUR
Editor, *Look;* President, 1968–69,
Sigma Delta Chi; Chairman, executive
committee, American Society of
Magazine Editors

EDWARD W. BARRETT
Director, Communications Institute,
Academy for Educational
Development, Inc.; former Dean,
Graduate School of Journalism,
Columbia University; former
Assistant Secretary of State

THOMAS WINSHIP
Editor, *Boston Globe*

AMERICAN COUNCIL ON EDUCATION MONOGRAPH

Special Commission on the Student Press

The Student Newspaper

Report of the Special Commission on the Student Press to the President of the University of California

Andrew S. Thomas Memorial Library
MORRIS HARVEY COLLEGE, CHARLESTON, W. VA.

AMERICAN COUNCIL ON EDUCATION
77120

378.198
Sp 3/s

© 1970 by American Council on Education
One Dupont Circle, Washington, D.C. 20036
Printed in the United States of America
Second impression November 1970
SBN 8268-1381-X
Library of Congress Catalog Card Number 72-121414

Contents

      Foreword   vii

      Letters of Transmittal   ix

      Charge   xi

      Prologue   xii

I   The Problem—and Its Scope   1

II   A History: From Land Grant to Tenure   7

III   *Jim Bettinger*
      Well, Mom, It Happened   12

IV   *Melvin Mencher*
      The College Newspaper   20

V   *John B. Wood*
      College Newspapers—Northeast   31

VI   *William Porter*
      What Should Be the Role of a Student Newspaper?   36

VII   *Arthur E. Sutton*
      A Few Thoughts on the Use
      of Obscenity by Campus Journalists   40

VIII   *John E. Moore*
      Reflections on Campus Press Problems   43

IX   The Commission's Recommendations   47

      Epilogue   57

Foreword

How effective are campus newspapers in meeting student needs? How should the student paper be financed and supervised? What is obscene language, and how should its use in campus publications be viewed? Is the student paper an "official" publication of the university?

These are some of the questions considered by the Special Commission on the Student Press appointed last year by the president of the University of California. The Commission, chaired by Norman E. Isaacs, president of the American Society of Newspaper Editors, specifically was asked to examine the student press on the campuses of the University of California. The Commission expanded its study to look at college journalism elsewhere in the nation before submitting a report at the end of the year.

Because of wide interest in the Commission's work, the University of California has permitted the American Council on Education to publish the report, making it available to other colleges and universities. The Council does not necessarily endorse the recommendations reached by the Commission and does not believe that all of the report's conclusions are applicable on all of the nation's campuses. The Council does commend the reading of the report to all of those in higher education who have responsibilities for student publications and who share the concerns expressed by the Commission.

Logan Wilson, *President*
American Council on Education

Letters of Transmittal

December 22, 1969

Dear President Hitch:

On behalf of the Special Commission on the Campus Press which you appointed last April, I have the privilege of submitting herewith the report which our group has now completed.

Please accept our apology for our inability to complete this report in time for the opening of the school year. Each of us, as you know, is deeply involved in other activities and it has often been difficult to coordinate our complicated schedules. Nevertheless, we have maintained an extremely close working relationship and we have consulted with each other at every step.

We cannot, in all candor, refer to this as an enjoyable or uplifting experience. Each of us recognized from the outset that the task posed perplexing problems. We accepted your call because, as professionals, we could not see ourselves turning away from what is a challenge to the whole of society. As we expected, we have frequently found ourselves searching our souls.

What we present here is the result of the most earnest study and not inconsiderable effort.

Sincerely,
Norman E. Isaacs
For the Special Commission

December 31, 1969

To The Regents of the University of California:

You will recall that The Regents requested at their March, 1969 meeting that I conduct a thorough investigation of all facets of campus publications. I reported at the May, 1969 meeting that I had named the following persons to a commission to assess the nature, role, and quality of student newspapers at the University campuses and to ascertain their degree of effectiveness in meeting student needs:

Norman Isaacs, President of the American Society of Newspaper Editors and Executive Editor of the Louisville *Courier-Journal* (Chairman)
Thomas Winship, Editor of the *Boston Globe*
Edward Barrett, former Dean of Columbia University's School of Journalism and currently with the Academy for Educational Development.
William Arthur, Editor of *Look* magazine and President of the Professional Journalistic Fraternity, Sigma Delta Chi

Enclosed is a copy of the report prepared by the commission. The report will be discussed at the January 15 meeting of the Committee on Educational Policy. Dean Edward Barrett will attend the meeting to present and answer questions on the report.

Charles J. Hitch

Charge

This Commission is respectfully asked to assess the nature, role, and quality of student newspapers at the University of California's campuses and ascertain their degree of effectiveness in meeting student needs. We would hope the study would include, but not be limited to, an appraisal of news and editorial content, quality of writing and reporting, and concepts of editorial policy. Consideration should be given to the fact that many student editors and reporters are not formally trained in basic journalism. The concept of a student newspaper should be explored: is it a training ground, a semiprofessional operation, or other type of enterprise? The possibility or need for a written code of performance should be examined. Attention should be given to the question of student support, with regard to financial viability, possible alternate means of financing, guarantees of freedom of the press, and other factors. The constitution of the Associated Students at each campus should be reviewed to determine the framework within which each paper functions. The committee should also consider various means of supervision by the university.

Prologue

Where men cannot freely convey their thoughts to one another, no freedom is secure. . . . Free expression is therefore unique among liberties: it promotes and protects all the rest. . . .

The freedom of the press illustrates the commonplace that if we are to live progressively we must live dangerously. . . .

The press is not free if those who operate it behave as though their position conferred on them the privilege of being deaf to ideas which the processes of free speech have brought to public attention. . . .

From the moral point of view, at least, freedom of expression does not include the right to lie as a deliberate instrument of policy.

The right of free public expression does include the right to be in error. Liberty is experimental. . . . What the moral right does not cover is the right to be deliberately or irresponsibly in error.

Commission on the Freedom of the Press
A Free and Responsible Press

1
The Problem—and Its Scope

Any study of student journalism leads inescapably to reflection of the larger scene: the total academic community and the atmosphere in which it serves.

Therefore, unless it is unconcerned, and, hence, irrelevant, student journalism cannot help but mirror to varying degrees prevailing campus moods.

In the nation's history, there have always been periods of reason and calm questioning, periods of constructive achievement, periods of anger and emotion.

The 1960s have been a period of torment for the United States. Riots and insurrection have swept many cities. An unpopular foreign war has divided the citizenry, contributed to inflation, wrecked political aspirations. Political assassination has shocked the public conscience.

While the mature generation of Americans has been uneasy, perplexed, and torn, much of the nation's youth has erupted into disorder. In many situations, challenge on campuses escalated into open revolt. (In the 1967–68 academic year, there were 221 demonstrations at 101 schools.) The language of communication has become debased. The evidence indicates that many students loyal to accepted, orderly processes have joined in supporting the indictment drawn by a vocally shrill minority.

This indictment accuses the older generation of resisting needed change; of hypocrisy between words and deeds; of racism; of supporting outmoded political patterns and methods; of pouring billions of dollars into arms while millions of human beings go hungry, uneducated, and unemployed.

The conflicts on these issues, and others, have been apparent in many nations and can be said to constitute virtually a worldwide trend.

Brought to the college and university campuses, the confrontation constitutes an emotionally charged "age-war."

Some studies of student unrest have appraised the problem in international terms (notably the Task Force on Violent Aspects of Protest and Confrontation in its research for the National Commission on the Causes and Prevention of Violence).

While the Task Force accepted the thesis that "the white student movement in America received inspiration in its early stages from dramatic

1

student uprisings in Japan, Turkey and South Korea" and that "French students were certainly inspired by the West Germans, and the Italians by the French," it concluded that "whatever similarity exists among student movements around the world is . . . neither completely spontaneous nor centrally coordinated."

Each generation cannot help but see the world through the prism of its own experiences. The older generation's conventional wisdom tends, therefore, to view campus life more in terms of a calmer period—of a teaching-and-learning process dominated by a sense of community and ordered discipline.

It is difficult for many older citizens to grasp the effects of the population explosion in the institutions of higher learning. The growth of enrollment has brought financial problems of vast proportions. In the 1968–69 academic year, there were almost seven million students enrolled in the nation's colleges and universities. Projections indicate that by 1977 these enrollments will have rocketed to just under ten million.

Nowhere is this student population explosion more graphically illustrated than in the University of California system. In the 1935–36 year, California had two major campuses (at Berkeley and Los Angeles), a new, smaller one (Davis), and the Medical Center. Total enrollment in the fall of 1935 was 20,669. In the 1958–59 year, with seven campuses, the enrollment had grown to 42,228. A decade later, in 1968–69 (nine campuses), the student population had more than doubled—to 96,695.

Clearly, the first major student rebellion in the United States was the "free speech" outburst in 1964. But protest movements, representing all the generations, were proliferating during the period.

Many of these protest groups adopted the weapon of defiant rudeness. The campus society, which has long cultivated the air of civility, was unprepared for this and acted both stunned and paralyzed. Determined protesters often found they could multiply the impact of their tactics by adding vulgarity and obscenity. Some argued that they were just overcoming adult hypocrisy.

At the outset, nonprotesting students, while dissenting, were clearly awed by the bravado of the abrasive maneuver.

However, when desperate administrations felt compelled to call in police to restore order, many moderate students and faculty members protested, holding this to be unwise reaction and a violation of what they considered campus immunity.

Though often among the more "responsible" elements, student journalists shared in and reflected these reactions, particularly on larger campuses. In some instances, student editors seemed affected by a desire to be in step with campus currents. They quickly discovered that the shock value of obscene words became doubly powerful in print. Across the nation, regents and trustees, presidents and chancellors, parents, alumni, and the general public counterreacted with indignation and protest of their own.

In this charged atmosphere, the University of California's Special Commission on the Student Press has endeavored over the past eight months to explore the problem dispassionately; to assess and gauge competence, effectiveness, and motive; to seek understanding of regental, administrative, faculty, and student goals and needs; and to seek paths leading to the protection of free expression consistent with journalistic responsibility and service.

It must be pointed out, in mentioning eight months of study, that it has been an undertaking to which its members could give only part time.

The study has included examination not only of the University of California's student publications but of campus journalism around the nation. The range in performance, frequency, quality, and sense of direction in these campus publications covers the entire spectrum—from high-caliber reporting and writing to slovenliness and inaccuracy; from obvious attempts to provide factual, basic news coverage for campus communities to equally patent drives to concentrate on causes dear to the hearts of individual staff members.

The methods of financing campus journals around the nation are equally wide-ranging—from totally independent publications to partial and, in some instances, total subsidy.

The principal, striking difference between the vast bulk of campus journalism and daily, commercial, professional journalism is what can only be termed the recognition on the professional level (and the corresponding nonrecognition by most student staffs) of interlocking authority. Each successful professional daily is a flexible web of authority, or authorities, operating as a team.

Campus journalism generally is afflicted by an absence of teamwork, training, or continuing counsel. Most college newspapers suffer from acute staffing shortages. The editors and managing editors tend to be "dedicated souls," often shorting academic work to insure publication of the campus newspapers.

Except in isolated cases, there has been little skilled counsel for editors and staffs. It is more or less a standard pattern for the aura of publishing legitimacy to be vested in boards of publications. These agencies, however, have generally veered away from exercising any but the loosest collaboration with editorial staffs and have concentrated on production and financing problems.

By and large, student journalists experience resistance from normal news sources in the university and college circles they attempt to cover; they receive faint praise for responsible performance and a steady stream of criticism for errors of judgment or execution.

Thus lacking skilled counseling, given either nothing or accorded stipends that often are among the lowest in campus scales, and left to operate in virtual vacuum, college editors more often than not have found themselves free of restraint, yet enslaved, forced to learn by doing.

Surprisingly, however, for all these difficulties and deficiencies, campus journalism around the nation continues to draw some of the brightest minds in the educational institutions, among the most devoted to a sense of duty and among the most determined to perform a community service.

In mid-July, the Newspaper Fund (established by the *Wall Street Journal*) reported that more than half of the nation's top high school students, the 1969 Presidential Scholars, had expressed strong interest in some form of journalistic or creative writing experience. Of the 121 Presidential Scholars, 65 had previously demonstrated an interest in journalism through work on school newspapers or in journalism courses. These interests clearly extend into the college years.

Being idealists, many of these student journalists gravitate toward intellectual association with what they conceive to be progressive causes. Lacking professional training, they sometimes fall into the errors of excessive subjective reporting; editorial comment becomes boringly strident; and some have reverted repeatedly to the shock techniques of four-letter language.

This is the national pattern. It is no worse and no better in the nine-campus system of the University of California.

Indeed, it can be said that the University of California's student press constitutes a small, but valid, cross section of the problems, uncertainties, range of guidance, and degrees of faculty indifference or neglect characterizing so much of the college journalism across the nation.

The Commission has consulted with deans and professors of journalism in many sections of the country and exchanged views with student editors and administrative officers in the California system.

The Commission encountered surprising extremes in each of the groups that constitute the unannounced antagonists.

Among student editors, it encountered able, deeply conscientious, and surprisingly professional individuals. It encountered others, happily a minority, who were basically no less worthy but who seemed confused about their role, unprofessional in such matters as simple fairness, and, on occasion, childish in efforts to attract attention. The best of the campus

THE PROBLEM 5

journalism examined was very good indeed. The worst was painfully amateurish and occasionally almost exhibitionist.

Among regents, the Commission talked with or heard from some who were clearly wise, tolerant, and cognizant of changes in society. It heard from others, also a minority, who seemed inflexible and in sympathy with antediluvian expressions voiced by some alumni, parents, and politicians. One regent inadvertently illustrated one of the problems. He joined in condemning campus press "obscenities," then, in a later informal moment, showed off a copy of his business club's burlesque newspaper, whose sex orientation and bawdiness at least equalled anything in the campus papers.

All the members of this Commission emerged with a sense of compassion for the system's administrators and chancellors who are often caught between the most extreme of regents and political figures on one hand and the most extreme of students (and sometimes faculty) on the other. The hope lies in the fact that there are in each group many individuals of reason, tolerance, and good will who can predominate if they choose to do so.

The Commission has elected to present its research and findings in the series of reports that follow. Some of the accompanying material was commissioned for this study, some has been taken directly from the campus journals.

The ensuing reports follow this sequence:[1]

Part II— A summation of the long-range trend in the University of California system ("A History: From Land Grant to Tenure," republished from the UCLA *Daily Bruin* of May 15, 1969)

Part III— A moving, personal testimonial by Jim Bettinger, Editor of the UC-Santa Barbara *El Gaucho* (republished from the edition of May 29, 1969)

Part IV— "The College Press," a summary of the state of campus journalism nationally (prepared for the Commission by Melvin Mencher, Associate Professor at the Graduate School of Journalism, Columbia University)

Part V— A report on the state of college newspapering in the northeastern portion of the United States (also prepared for the Commission by John B. Wood, 1968–69 Managing Editor of the *Yale Daily News*)

Part VI— A personalized, slightly whimsical, incisive review of "What Should Be the Role of a Student Newspaper?" by William

1. The Commission's presentation included excerpts from the report of the Task Force on Violent Aspects of Protest and Confrontation to the National Commission on the Causes and Prevention of Violence. These excerpts are not included in this printed version.

Porter, Chairman of the Journalism Department at the University of Michigan

Part VII— A forthright review of the obscene language problem ("A Few Thoughts on the Use of Obscenity by Campus Journalists," provided to the Commission by Arthur E. Sutton, Special Assistant to the Chancellor, UC-Riverside, July 28, 1969)

Part VIII— An overview of the general campus publication issues (by John E. Moore, Faculty Representative, UC-Santa Barbara Communications Board, August 12, 1969)

Part IX— The Commission's recommendations.

II
A History:
From Land Grant to Tenure

Eldridge Cleaver, tuition, fee increases, ROTC, ethnic studies, budget cuts from Sacramento, faculty tenure appointment power—these are the controversies which have faced the UC Board of Regents through student activism for the past four or five years.

Most observers trace today's campus turmoil to the 1964 Free Speech Movement at UC Berkeley. Many are either too young or have forgotten the loyalty oath controversy of 1950, which some regents claim was even more serious a crisis for the University than FSM.

Actually, the current situation stems in part from two historical occurrences: UC becoming a land grant college in 1864—taking on the accompanying obligations to the federal government involving military training on campus and strings attached to federal funds—and World War II and its relationship to public service and war-related research.

Signed into law by Abraham Lincoln in 1862, the Morrill Land Grant Act stimulated the creation or development of the 68 colleges and universities in the United States now referred to as land grant colleges.

The measure granted 30,000 acres of public land to each state for each of its senators and representatives in Congress as apportioned by the 1860 census. California was thus entitled to 150,000 acres.

The Morrill Act required acceptance of land grants by the states within two years after its passage. It also required that states accepting the grants must establish at least one college "where the leading object shall be, without excluding other scientific and classical studies, and including military tactics, to teach such branches of learning as are related to agriculture and the mechanical arts, in such manner as the Legislature of the States may respectively prescribe..."

In response to claims and demands by dissidents that ROTC should be abolished on campus, administrators often cite the Morrill Act as proof the University is legally obligated to the federal government to maintain ROTC on at least one campus of the University.

Reprinted from the University of California, Los Angeles, *Daily Bruin*, 15 May 1969, by permission of the Communications Board of the Associated Students of the University of California, Los Angeles.

Similarly, the foundation was laid in World War II for the current criticism of war related research on campus.

As the War pre-empted the normal functions of the University and the government poured unprecedented funds for war research into institutions of higher education, new and government-based research became king.

One might have expected a return to the peace time educational direction of such institutions after the war had ended. But to this day, such research has played an increasingly dominant role.

In the past, federal grants were often given to a professor to allow him to "do his own thing." While this is true today, federal grants are often associated with government-directed research, much of it related to national security. In the long run, the emphasis on research in and of itself has increased tremendously, at an often admitted cost to teaching.

By 1950 the stage had been set for the first political repercussions that struck the Regents with unprecedented force and tore at the very heart of the University: the students and the faculty.

The Regents, in the summer of 1950, voted to require all University employees to sign a loyalty oath, after much public debate and political pressure. The Regents fired 32 professors who refused to sign, and many more resigned in protest before being fired.

Three men here, assistant physics prof. David Saxon, history prof. John Caughey and associate history prof. Charles Mow refused to sign the oath.

Saxon, now vice chancellor here, said at the time:

"By their action of August 25, in which they rejected the recommendations of President (Robert Gordon) Sproul and the Faculty Committee on Privilege and Tenure, a bare majority (12–10) of the Board of Regents has challenged the very basis of academic self-government, that is the right of the faculty itself to decide on the qualifications of its members."

Those were the days when Admiral Chester William Nimitz, John E. Canaday and Edwin W. Pauley (both regents) and Earl Warren served on the Board.

ROTC first became a big issue involving the Regents during the spring semester of 1962. After months of debate and consultations with the Defense Dept., the Regents voted unanimously to end compulsory military training for lower division students.

The Regents on the same date received 4745 signatures of faculty, students and employees urging them to relinquish "censorship powers over selection of campus speakers."

The Board of Regents finally voted to lift its ban on Communist speakers in June 1963. The removal of the ban, in effect since 1951, was recommended to the Regents by UC President Clark Kerr and approved 15–2–1 following the defeat of an amendment by Regent John E. Canaday.

The new policy, as approved, allowed any off-campus speakers to speak on University campuses, but provided that "whenever the respective Chancellor considers it appropriate in furtherance of educational objectives, he may require any or all of the following:

- That the meeting be chaired by a tenure faculty member;
- That the speaker be subject to questions from the audience;
- That the speaker be appropriately balanced in debate with a person of contrary opinions."

The new campus speaker ruling was no match for the situation at Berkeley, where students were soliciting funds for off-campus political causes and demanding the right to speak and distribute literature whenever and wherever they wanted to on campus.

The result was the now infamous Free Speech Movement, which is still reverberating across the nation.

After demonstrations and near-riots through October and November, 1964, the Regents voted to change official policy to allow solicitation of funds and volunteers on campus for lawful off-campus political and social activity.

Under the new regulation, however, a student involved in an illegal off-campus act planned on campus, such as advocacy of civil disobedience in a civil rights demonstration, would be subject to discipline by the University administration.

FSM immediately called the new regulation unconstitutional and held "illegal" rallies the next day.

At the same time, the Regents created still another controversy by approving plans for a football stadium here to be constructed with student fees.

Politics soon entered the picture when then State Sen. Thomas M. Rees, now Democratic Congressman from the 26th Congressional District, charged that the proposed stadium was a "shocking extravagance" at a time when qualified students are not able to attend the college due to a lack of funds since there is a widespread revolt among taxpayers.

The administration replied that the stadium was not being built with taxpayers' money, and Rees replied, "I think this is a bunch of baloney."

Back to FSM; on Dec. 4 over 800 students staged a sit-in in Berkeley's Sproul Hall and were arrested by order of ex-officio Regent Gov. Edmund G. Brown.

The same week a *Daily Bruin* poll showed that 66.7 per cent of the students questioned here were opposed to FSM actions at Berkeley.

Back to the proposed football stadium; the following March, 1965, 2200 students organized against the stadium and circulated petitions stating that student fees should not be used for its construction.

A student referendum held March 11 and 12 showed students to be opposed to the football stadium 2417–1002.

The FSM still going strong; the Regents heard two reports from two of their own committees on the movement in May. One report, authored by Regent Theodore Meyer, called for stringent student regulations. The other report, submitted by Robert Byrne (he was hired for the investigation by a regental committee headed by Regent William Forbes) proposed that students be given a broader voice in determining the policies of the University.

UC President Clark Kerr, who had resigned once during the FSM trouble at Berkeley but later decided to keep his post, was soon at loggerheads with newly elected Gov. Ronald Reagan in January 1967. Reagan had proposed an investigation of the University and a $400 per year tuition, and Kerr had vigorously dissented.

The result: On Friday, Jan. 20, 1967, the Regents voted 14–8 to fire Kerr from his job.

Kerr blamed partisan politics for his ouster.

Mrs. Catherine Hearst, who voted to dismiss Kerr, said "he had a lack of administrative ability."

Governor Ronald Reagan, who left an hour before the announcement of Kerr's firing was made, called the action "very reasonable."

The reaction to the Regents' decision was one of shock and anger on UC campuses throughout the state. UCLA students, 8000 strong, marched in protest and held a mass rally in Pauley Pavilion.

1968 was a crisis year for the Regents, with tuition talk and the initiation of large-scale anti-regent demonstrations at the monthly meetings.

The tuition crisis is now history—at least that phase of it. An $81 fee increase was approved in April, at UC Davis after 15 months of heated debate and anxious waiting on the part of students.

The meeting at Davis also marked the first serious anti-regent demonstrations. About 600 Davis students jammed the gymnasium-auditorium and presented a list of demands to the Regents concerning minority education. The sponsoring group: the Martin Luther King Coalition.

The Regents agreed to look into the area of minority student problems and also earmarked some of the money expected to result from increased students fees to student scholarships and financial aid.

Eldridge Cleaver became one of the most controversial men in California history when Gov. Reagan publicly criticized the University for letting Cleaver schedule a series of 10 classroom lectures for an experimental course on racism at Berkeley.

Meeting here in September, the Regents passed a resolution, 10–8, limiting all guest lecturers to one appearance in credit classes.

A vote against the resolution might mean, in this case, that a Regent felt Cleaver should not be allowed to speak even once.

Protests at Berkeley followed, and student pressure was kept up until the following November at San Diego where the Regents voted to allow each campus chancellor to make exceptions to the one lecture ruling.

Cleaver, however, gave "articulate" lectures in course 139X as Berkeley students fought to obtain course credit for it after the Regents had voted to ban credit from the class.

In the meantime, Cleaver kept up a heavy speaking schedule that included a stop in Pauley Pavilion where he told students "if you're not part of the solution, then you're part of the problem."

At the February meeting in Berkeley, in the midst of tear gas and riot squads called into action in response to the Third World Liberation Front Strike, the Regents passed restrictive measures involving mandatory penalties for law violators.

At the March meeting here, the Regents adopted a resolution introduced by Regent Canaday calling for an investigation into all the UC campus newspapers and an investigation into the use of non-voluntary student fees for support of the newspapers and other political activities.

A report of the finds of the latter investigation into campus newspapers will probably not be completed until sometime later this year according to UC administrators.

In one of the most significant regental actions in years, the Board voted 13–10–1 at Berkeley last month to revoke the chancellors' authority over tenure faculty appointments and promotions and return it to the Regents.

The action was received negatively by the faculty here and around the state, and the UC chancellors, who had conducted a vigorous campaign against the action, expressed disappointment and/or anger.

The fact that the resolution was amended to say no political test would be used in determining appointments seemed to indicate a fear of political intervention despite those who took the amendment at face value.

At the meeting Hitch came out reluctantly in favor of increased student fees or tuition, providing the money would be used for campus construction, that part of the University's budget most severely cut by Reagan.

A study of tuition was ordered for next month's meeting in San Francisco at the same time.

III Jim Bettinger
Well, Mom, It Happened

Well, mom, it happened. You remember how you told me that I damn well wasn't going to Berkeley after the Free Speech Movement? How I was going to go down to that nice little beach school where all the responsible parents were sending their kids and where Kirk Douglas sent his son and where the fraternities and sororities taught people how to behave and where there weren't any demonstrations and how it was becoming a socially important school and what a beautiful Spanish town Santa Barbara was and how you wouldn't have to worry about me while I was here? Well, mom, it happened.

It happened to a lot of us. It happened to a whole educational generation—the generation of students who were seniors in high school when Berkeley broke wide open for the first time four-and-a-half years ago.

We are, in large part, the result of our parents' fears for us. And we are also, in large part, the result of our own fears, because Berkeley was something that we weren't sure we could handle.

We had this wonderful image of college—the Ozzie Nelson fun-time image, where you went to classes and then everybody bopped down to ogle each other at the malt shoppe where Pop (everybody called him Pop) served sodas.

And maybe if there was nothing else to do, like root the freshman squash team on, or wander through the student store trying on sweatshirts, you might talk to someone about things that could happen after next Saturday night, or you just might study, even though David and Ricky didn't have to. You just might.

And of course everyone—but everyone—wore blue cardigans and sharp khakis and a white dress shirt, open at the neck, and scuffed white bucks. The girls (they were never women) belonged in toothpaste ads—the old kind, when mouths didn't have sex appeal and brassy chicks didn't go around throwing kisses at guys in armor plate.

Jim Bettinger, Editor, University of California, Santa Barbara, *El Gaucho*.
Reprinted from the University of California, Santa Barbara, *El Gaucho*, 29 May 1969, by permission of the author.

For better or worse, this was the way we saw college. Even after Berkeley in 1964, we thought the rest of the schools had stayed the same, that only Berkeley, with its beatniks and pinkos, had changed.

This was the way our parents saw college, too. Those parents who were college educated came along during the late 1930's or early 1940's when going to college was really a privilege, because you were either escaping the Depression or escaping the War.

And in those days, college really was a place where you could get away from the social reality of a scared country. We had just had our confidence in capitalism shaken to the core, and now we were being attacked by the vilest war criminal the world had ever seen.

The colleges and universities had not yet taken their loyalty oaths to the nation. The military had not yet discovered that in the laboratories of American education there resided a treasure trove of unimagined utility. We were still free of its financial resources as well.

Those of us whose parents did not go to college know even more graphically the effect economic disaster had upon them. Perhaps none of them will ever quite be able to escape the feeling that apple stands are just around the corner.

Yet we came from an affluent society—the most affluent man has ever known. We had our own cars, our own television sets, full wardrobes of clothes; we controlled major industries with our buying habits. Rock 'n' roll had never sold to anyone over 20, let alone anyone over 30.

So we came to college, in large part, not for any overriding goal of intellectual achievement, but more because it was the final step in our socialization process. We were to go through the ritual of four years' duration so that when the University spit us out in 1969, we would be able to take our place in society as full citizens. We wouldn't be educated, we would be confirmed. We would be quality controlled.

But somewhere along the way, quality control misfired. Instead of turning out progressively more consuming and complacent junior executives, the system is turning out progressively angrier, progressively more skeptical students. It started four years ago, and it will continue to do so until there is a drastic change in the priorities of our society. And all the cries for "lawnorder" in the world can't change this basic fact.

Why is this taking place? Why is the most affluent, the apparently most free, the seemingly most progressive society getting deep dissatisfaction out of its institutions of higher education? Closer to home, why are we discontent (or as some would call us, malcontent)? What has led to our specific and general dissatisfaction with American life and society?

Never has it been easier to enrage students than it is today. After more demonstrations than I care to count, I come away sobered by the depth of feeling the students who take part in these demonstrations and disruptions have. It is almost a feeling that logic has failed, reason has failed, the channels have failed. It is a feeling that the only moral thing left to do is to shout at the system, for if you shout at it, at least it has to pay attention to you. If you shout at it, at least you will have cleared your conscience.

It is a very pessimistic and sometimes very anti-human feeling. A feeling that there is really no humanity left to respect. It is a feeling one might expect to come from a person being physically tortured and, finally being able to stand it no longer, who gives a last cry of defiance before his tormentors do away with him.

The big problem is that our parents, our schools and our churches told us to be idealists. If they had never mentioned the Declaration of Independence, there would be much less student unrest today.

Our ideals can remain important to us only if they withstand the test of reality. They can remain strong only if we feel that we can work toward them, and many students feel that there is no chance of this left.

The second big problem is that the University made a decision, perhaps unconsciously, to try to deal with reality. It made some small decision somewhere—perhaps it was not even considered a decision at the time—to lay its idealism on the line and see how relevant it was.

And things went along well for awhile, because the first area in which it tried to become relevant was national defense and industry. In this area, the scientific expertise of the ivy-covered colony was of premium value. It wasn't political, because no one could argue against defending the country. It wasn't radical, because it fit in with our national hardware store philosophy of national security.

(If we can't convince those commie bastards that we're right, we can at least blind them with the glare from our Nikes. And then we can blow them up.)

The decision threatened nothing in American society, and, in the last analysis, this meant that it would never be severely questioned. Oh, there were a few fellow-traveler scientists who worried about whether a man had to take responsibility for weapons he had created but over which he had no control, but for the most part, the Edward Tellers prevailed and others quickly learned that without money, you can't do one hell of a lot of research.

And then came the blacks. Along came Jones, and he wasn't sweet-talking white America at all. Ten years later the country was in an upheaval.

The blacks, more than anyone else, jolted America's moral senses. While they were invisible, whites could ignore them to a large extent. They could speak freely about the freedom in America, because it was not within the realm of their experience to consider the degradation of black America.

But the blacks became visible, and suddenly all the talk about the land of the free was just that—talk. Politicians, editorialists, preachers and businessmen sounded more and more irrelevant when they soared to the heights of patriotic rhetoric.

The Civil Rights Movement was only the start. The North could look at the South and cluck its tongue over how terrible the situation "down there" was. It could wonder how any area could allow the Ku Klux Klan, the White Citizens' Councils, and the overt racism that was displayed in the segregation laws.

And in 1964, then-Governor of Alabama George Corley Wallace polled 34 per cent of the Democratic primary vote in Wisconsin, 30 per cent in Indiana, 43 per cent in Maryland, and the myth was shattered. Racism was everywhere.

In that year, too, the riverboat gambler from Texas (by this time operating from Capitol Hill) decisively defeated the rugged reactionary from Arizona by running, at least in part, on a peace platform. Our generation graduated from high school four months after he had started bombing North Vietnam to show how serious he was about his quest for peace.

So the males of our generation always had the war in Vietnam hanging over their heads, and with it, the draft. At first, one always had to identify which war he had in mind; after a while, it became simply The War.

The draft, meanwhile, did more to keep college enrollment up to par than any economic or intellectual incentive. Every time during those years that we felt we weren't learning anything, that we were becoming increasingly irrelevant to our society, that we wanted out, all we had to do was take out our wallet, look at the little card with its II-S that said, "Do Not Disturb," and remember how lucky we were that we wouldn't have to transfer our fraternity affiliation to that new house, the Mekong Delts.

The War kept us from leaving the University for reality, but it couldn't keep us from trying to bring reality to the University. This generation of college students has been more concerned with, and more effective in, using its own spare time and energy in social activism than any other previous generation.

It is amazing that we should take for granted the efforts of our fellow students. 1900 of them have worked this year through the facilities of the Community Affairs Board, tutoring, working with the youth of Goleta, raising funds for Camp Conestoga, and organizing a number of other projects for the direct benefit of both the campus and the wider community.

But there was more to it than just going out to the community for service projects. There was also an attempt to bring society to the University, with speakers, seminars and special events. We felt isolated out here—we felt like we could too easily forget there was an outside world.

And the blacks and chicanos kept coming, brought here by a University and federal program (EOP) but ultimately responsible only to themselves and their communities.

A lot of us didn't like what they were saying. We tried to make Black Power what Nixon is trying to make it—economic tokenism. And, as they confronted us with the realities of the ghetto, we reacted in one of two ways —we either took the white liberal burden of guilt and agreed with everything they said, or we defensively took a conservative stand and agreed with nothing they said. The people who were willing to do more than just agree or disagree were rare birds.

It was hard not to play white liberal. There was no way we could escape the degradation of black America, and sometimes we thought that by agreeing with their analysis, we had somehow "become black," that we were therefore entitled to speak for the blacks. We talked a lot about revolution.

And it was easy to be defensive. The blacks were attacking us on our home grounds, and we felt human enough and had been weaned enough so that we felt that fighting back when attacked was the honest thing to do. We talked a lot about opportunities.

And when it came right down to it, we didn't do a damn thing, because we still really didn't know our selves. We were still afraid to make that commitment because we couldn't know what the consequences might be. We didn't know what this commitment might require of us. We wanted so much to say that we had not compromised our ideals, and that is one helluva lot easier to do if you don't have any.

We were willing to go to rallies, to be sure, and we were willing to sign petitions for any worthwhile cause, but we were unwilling, for the most part, to really dig into the situation and find out what could be done.

The administration was handy, so we confronted it. We were angry, but we never stopped to think why we were angry. We thought we knew, but we never could have been more wrong.

John F. Kennedy said once that "those who make peaceful revolution impossible, make violent revolution inevitable." If violent revolution is inevitable, then it is we who have made the peaceful revolution impossible.

Because, all that the blacks and chicanos were really asking for was to be treated like real human beings with economic, social and educational needs which are basically the same as all mankind's. We refused to do that —our white liberal guilt was based on the premise that they were different and were to be treated as such. And the guiltiest are those who profess their liberality and sympathy the most. Methinks the revolutionary doth protest too much.

And on the other side, those of us who reacted defensively simply could not see the problems which the blacks and chicanos faced. Wrapped up in our own smug sensibilities, we never really understood why they didn't want to do things on our terms, why they mistrusted the channels.

We have spent the last four years confused. We have done our little bit for society, with our tutoring projects and our service clubs and, yes, our newspapering, but we have never really understood why. And maybe this is a partial reason for the rage we sometimes feel.

But there are other reasons, too. There is this tremendous feeling that no one is in control of anything. We are not in control of our own lives— and we can't find who is.

It is as if we have created some technological juggernaut which is running roughshod over all our human frailties and capabilities. You can wake up sweating some nights thinking that all the computers in the world have hooked up together with telephone lines (courtesy of Bell Telephone's scientific progress) and our massive communications complex is about to annihilate us.

As the society grows larger and more diverse, our technology grows larger and more unified. The answer for most people is a rehumanization of our social contacts, to make us believe that each of us really has something unique inside.

A second answer is to lose oneself in the growing morass of information, so that one becomes responsive, not to other people, but to charts, graphs, books, and the pyrex jungle of a laboratory.

For still others, the answer is simply to destroy the technology—perhaps humanity is not quite ready to use our knowledge effectively (except in the killing of other humans). If the tools escalate man's Stone Age emotions, then maybe the elimination of them will prevent his emotions from destroying him.

Perhaps the real answer is a combination of the first two possibilities. The joining of humanism and technology would seem to be the same theme as the original Renaissance, and could possibly have an even greater effect upon civilization. But, of course, here one has to watch out for an overdone emphasis: an emotional technology or a technological emotionality are both contradictions in terms.

All of which leaves us where we started: confused.

EL GAUCHO has been in the middle of this confusion all year. We have at times been the guilty white liberal, the smug reactionary, the white radical, the harried student, the hassled administrator, the removed faculty member, and the frightened human being.

Newspapers are of course technological, and they more often than not tend to fall into the category of being responsive only to information and not to people. We said at the start of the year that we were going to try to change that to a certain extent: "To communicate through symbols is one of the most human things a person can do. We expect to be a very human newspaper."

But to say one is going to communicate and to actually communicate effectively are two very different matters. Communication is a very fragile phenomenon, depending upon trust, clarity, perception, interest, and a very nebulous area called "common ground." The German poet Goethe once said of a poet that "as long as he expresses only these few subjective sentences he can not yet be called a poet, but as soon as he knows how to appropriate the world for himself, and to express it, he is a poet."

This is what writers of all kinds are trying to do deep down. Newspapers are really only a medium for this appropriation and expression—and out of that medium has grown a whole other standard, objectivity. To the extent that objectivity helps facilitate this expression of the world, it is valuable, though objectivity is not an end in itself.

But have we been a human newspaper? That is a difficult thing to discern, for while we have felt sometimes that the medium did not allow us to express ourselves openly, most of us have never felt dehumanized by it.

There is another matter, and that is the trust that many people put in a newspaper. They put that trust there because they largely believe us, and to the small extent that EL GAUCHO starts out with this trust each year, it is a good thing. But trust, once again, is a fragile thing; it only takes a few small mistakes (or one major one) to taint it beyond repair. There is that element of humanity in the paper, the need to be respected.

And there are other elements, too. We felt that this year was, above all, confusing—there were never any easy decisions to make, and we felt that we had to convey this element of student thought as well as the others. Perhaps we emphasized this element too much, but events have a way of doing that to people.

Early in September, then-City Editor Rick Roth said that "there's going to be a time this year when everyone around us is going to be losing their heads, and we're going to have to keep ours." (Rick also noted the other side of this analysis: "If you can keep your head while all around you are losing theirs, then maybe you aren't very cognizant of the situation.") We picked the first analysis, and tried to stick to it all year. Whether or not this was the right decision, only time will tell. We are proud of it.

And so we leave 1400-odd pages of Vol. 49 to gather dust on the shelf. They will be referred to only for minor statistics ("How many votes did Knell get last year?") and the amusement of the staff, which will find our little labor of love rich with technical and philosophical errors. So be it.

But future staffs will also know, because they are themselves involved in the day-to-day grind of producing a relevant and factual newspaper, that we took our work seriously. For many of us, EL GAUCHO has been our education in the realities of sociology, politics, and psychology. We wouldn't trade it for the world.

And now we leave, most of us for the big bad world, where there are no professors, no students, and the University is a dirty word. Some of us will take our places quietly, but most will take their places not so quietly, for the experience gained there has taught us that a dream is worth fighting for and maybe dying for.

Peace, brothers and sisters.

IV
Melvin Mencher

The College Newspaper

The reasons usually advanced for the existence of a student newspaper are concerned with its utility. Where there are journalism programs, the newspaper is a good training ground for the journalism major. In general, the newspaper is supposed to function as a source of information and as an aid in the development of the consensus necessary to make the campus function properly.

Elsewhere on the campus, the fraternal social system deals with social and housing matters. Various clubs and organizations give students an opportunity to be of service to the university and provide an outlet for student energy.

Unlike these activities, the campus newspaper exposes students to a profession or trade with an ethic and a loyalty of its own. In their practice of journalism, students often move beyond the service function that the institution sets for them.

At the simplest level, the institution expects basic information from the newspaper, the "bulletin board" function. It seeks from the newspaper the who, what, when, and where of the clubs, faculty activities, and administrative actions.

But the student journalist, who looks off the campus for his models, has other ideas. He sees a journalism grown uneasy with its heritage of the objective coverage of overt events. Seeking his rewards in the profession, should he be a journalism major, he patterns himself on the successful reporter and editor.

The professional journalist's task is to serve his readers, not the news source. And this is the cause of much of the consternation on the campus. The student journalist sees his readers as students, not as administrators, parents, legislators, politicians, alumni. The nonstudents are the people whose activities he scrutinizes, particularly administrators.

On the other hand, the administrator sees the student press much as he views other campus service groups. Whatever the reason for this attitude toward the student newspaper, it permeates and poisons the relationship between the university and the student newspaper.

Melvin Mencher, Associate Professor of Journalism, Columbia University.

THE COLLEGE NEWSPAPER   21

The student who takes his journalism seriously views himself as a professional man seeking the truth from sources reluctant to give him adequate information. He sees himself as the Washington reporter prying information from a congressman or a city hall reporter digging into the mayor's personal business activities. (See the *Michigan Daily*'s stories about the questionable activities of a university regent and its exposure of the business actions of the president of Michigan State University and several of his university colleagues.)

The source—most often an administrator, although the faculty nowadays is being scrutinized for its relationship with the "military-industrial complex"—rebels at this intrusion, and a state of tension develops. Although this is seen on the campus as an unusual situation, this tension between journalist and news source is a normal one. Indeed, journalism can be defined as the art of gathering information from sources reluctant to disclose what they know.

The campus newspaper that engages its reporters and editors in the journalistic process provides them with an educational experience worthy of the students' investment of time and energy.

The newspaper that gives young men and women this experience nurtures independence, maturity, and responsibility. It teaches young men and women to investigate before they accept ready-made solutions. Serving on a student newspaper that is free to examine issues and then to draw its conclusions is a small but sure step away from the pressures on youth to accept, to be passive, to go along. Few students seem interested in confronting the overwhelming forces around them. Nothing, they say, can be done. Others, equally passive, bury themselves in social theory, and in the great movements of history, never facing the human ache and misery under these tides. Not most student newsmen. They and other action-oriented students in the past decade have been leaders in the struggle for civil rights. They widened the debate on U.S. foreign policy so that, for example, opposition to the war in Vietnam became an acceptable point of view, and they initiated major reforms in higher education. For the past decade the campus newsman has been more than a mild tug at the campus conscience.

Except for a few campuses, the student newspaper today is more passive than its predecessors. It is the victim of spiritual malaise, mistaken loyalty, and administrative headhunting. On the campuses where it still thrives, administrators are pursuing it relentlessly. They will probably succeed; but the victory will be hollow, for the student newspaper is not the real prey they hunt, only the nearest at hand.

Until fairly recently the student newspaper was where the action was on campus. Its editors were the predecessors of today's activists and dissidents. No one can understand the condition of the student press today without examining its past.

Recent History

Several threads run through this twenty-five-year history. One obvious strand is the seriousness with which the student journalist took the responsibility of the intellectual to improve his society. Parallel to that commitment is the faith he placed in his professors and the university as the institution above all others that sought truth.

When he listened to lectures about democracy and saw the fraternal groups practicing the crudest kind of discrimination, he was appalled and said so. When his teachers examined the history of this country's foreign relations, the student editor was led to speak out on the nation's approach to Cuba, Communist China, and the Soviet Union.

In other words, the student journalist was broadcasting to a wide audience much of what he heard in the classroom. The campus press had broken the gentleman's agreement that keeps the public outside the wall. Parents, legislators, politicians, and others had heretofore been privy to the fortunes of the basketball team, developments in contour plowing, and open-heart surgery. But the campus newspaper changed that blissful relationship.

It opened the classroom to the public.

And everyone ran for cover in the ensuing storm. The faculty, never too happy with the disinterest of the student press in its accomplishments, recoiled.

Journalism teachers, most of whom had formal arrangements with the student newspaper, wanted out. Administrators, sensing alumni and political reaction, moved in.

Off the campus, the pressures on youth were accumulating: the Vietnam War, the draft, and increasingly violent racial confrontations. There seemed to be little that youth could do to control what it felt was a deteriorating situation.

The deterioration was not the result of the know-nothings in the society but of the very people youths in the past had trusted as the keepers of the liberal tradition.

The student journalist knows he has been deserted by his professors. Indeed, the round of demonstrations on campuses in 1968 and 1969 was directed as much at faculty careerists as at aloof administrators. The student knows that he is the most convenient scapegoat for the faculty and the administration when they seek to placate those pounding on the walls of academe.

He has been saying for several years that tossing his skull to the headhunters is foolish, for they hunt for meatier game. He has been trying to say that the university is as obligated to his freedom as it is to the teacher's and that once freedom is constricted in the newsroom the classroom might be next.

Journalists React

Few listened to his pleas to end discrimination on the campus, to give minority groups off campus decency and dignity. He embarrassed the university by urging moderation in the examination of Cuba, China and the Soviet Union. He sought consideration for the plight of the student forced into antihuman dormitories, marshalled into rows of hundreds for classes, ignored by self-seeking faculty members, and, in short, treated like automatons seeking only a piece of paper at the end of the assembly line.

Little wonder student journalists became strident and that their readers moved onto picket lines and then into offices. Kenneth Keniston, associate professor of psychology at Yale, summed up the situation:

"The increasing tendency of students to use disruptive tactics partly springs from their conviction that they simply have no other way to make their opinions heard and felt."

When writers are frustrated in communicating, they seek extremes of language to shock their readers into a realization of the situation. They meet obscenity with obscenity. As many editors have said, there is no four-letter word as obscene as the Vietnam War.

Regents, administrators, trustees, and even faculty move in, seizing upon the most recent display of linguistic extreme, refusing to face up to causes.

This reaction is not new to student journalists. Dozens of cases could be cited where editors were reprimanded, dismissed, even placed on probation for extremes of expression—extreme in idea and/or in language. At UCLA a few years ago, a literary supplement contained some material from a William Burroughs novel and a mordant drawing by George Grosz, the German artist. These were legitimate expressions of a distaste with society. But off-campus keepers of morality were appalled. Mayor Yorty sent the vice squad to investigate. The Santa Monica newspaper carried front-page stories. The situation became so difficult that Dr. Franklin Murphy advised the staff that the only solution was to discharge the editor so that he could appease the attackers. The publications board resisted and the editor agreed to issue an apology.

Looking back the few years to that incident, we cannot get excited about the words and pictures that so excited the vigilantes. Tomorrow, we will be passing the same judgment on what exercises the community today.

Selection and Removal of the Editor

The selection of an editor is of prime importance to the staff, which seeks continuity of editorial and news policies. A former editor at the University of Colorado said his major regret was not any editorial failure but his failure to "politick my man through as editor."

At the University of San Francisco in 1964, the staff of the award-winning weekly, the *Foghorn,* quit in protest when the dean of students pushed through the Publications Council a new editor. The twenty-five staffers who resigned said the new editor was the dean's man and might "lower the pressure" on the administration, with which the newspaper had often disagreed.

At the University of Texas, where editors are elected by the student body, the election by the student body in 1966 of a conservative student outside the *Texan*'s inner group of political liberals split the staff. The successful candidate ran on a pro-Vietnam War platform.

Many methods are used in the selection of the editor. They range from all-campus elections to the outgoing editor's selection of his successor. In some institutions, the staff elects the editor. In a few, an administrator appoints the editor. Most often, the publications board selects the editor from nominating petitions presented it.

In recent years, the all-campus election of editors has been initiated by administrators seeking to blunt the liberal-radical edge of the newspaper. When newspaper policy is subject to student endorsement, the editor becomes involved in a popularity contest. Few students prefer the candidate who promises to become the campus conscience. Editors are almost unanimous in their criticism of this device. Some blame it for the drastic changes, most often for the worse, in the performance of newspapers.

The nomination by the staff and appointment by the publications board, which guarantees a continuance of policy, can encourage control of the newspaper by cliques. But to most editors, the risks are greater in other systems.

Editors usually may be removed by the group (e.g., publications board) that administers the newspaper; although ultimate authority, except where the newspaper is separately incorporated, rests with the president of the institution. In a few cases, referendum machinery exists for the recall of an editor.

Removal of an editor for incompetence is unusual. Student-faculty boards of publications, the staffs themselves, and the other groups that administer the newspaper usually choose a person who appears to them to be competent. When difficulties arise, the staff is likely to handle the problem internally, moving another editor into the top post with no fanfare. Boards are prone to discuss the issue with the editor, warn him if necessary, but take no precipitate action.

An editor's removal should be considered by the body that elected or appointed him, and the final decision should be made by the same group. A board can be useful to an administrator badgered by off-campus critics. He can stave off attack by telling them the board is empowered to act, not he.

The news staff and the publications board are less receptive to the off-campus influences that move presidents to act against editors. Nor are they as concerned over the image of the institution as the administrator. In fact, they often present a front with the editor against such administrative pressures and may tend to keep an incompetent editor on the masthead too long.

Where the publications board has a large number of representatives of student government, there is built-in trouble. The newspaper then is being watched by the people it is policing. When it is brought before the board, the newspaper often is judged by its accusers.

The university president on almost all campuses has the ultimate power to dismiss an editor. When he uses this power to step over the regular authorities, as in 1962 at the University of Colorado, or where he orders the board to act, as in 1966 at the University of Florida, there is a furor.

Asked to list the actions of editor that might lead them to intervene (in a survey I conducted) presidents gave the following grounds:

Printing overly critical materials
Violating rules of good taste
Irresponsibility
Insubordination

These differ markedly from the most frequently listed causes given by members of publications boards and advisers for dismissal. They listed:

Incompetence
Failure to abide by formal regulations such as a stipulated grade average
Conviction in a libel suit
Grave personal misconduct

The Adviser

Every newspaper should have an adviser, paid out of the newspaper's funds. The staff should do the hiring. The adviser should not be a member of the faculty but should preferably be a reporter or editor from a nearby newspaper. His function should be that of instructor-critic. He should function as adviser, not prepublication censor, offering advice when asked. His postpublication function should be to critique the newspaper.

Sponsorship

The newspaper should not be the laboratory product of the school or department of journalism. This places the newspaper under the control of the journalism school, which is sensitive to pressure from the university.

Financing the Newspaper

The cost of publishing the college newspaper has increased steadily, and revenues have not kept pace. To make ends meet, an increasing amount of space has had to be devoted to advertising, which means fewer inches for news and comment which, in turn, creates dissatisfied readers. Business managers have saved money by examining alternative printing processes. The trend to offset has been steady.

Eighty percent of the college newspapers are financed by a subsidy or through the allocation of a portion of the mandatory student fee.

Twenty percent of the daily college newspapers do not operate on a set fee from students or on a subsidy but are financed through circulation and advertising revenue. Two-thirds or more of their income comes from advertising.

Many of the daily newspapers, whatever their original financing arrangement, have had to seek subsidies from their schools to meet rising costs. When the newspaper is subsidized, the editor usually agrees to distribute the newspaper free to all students.

The newspapers that rely for income on cash subscriptions and newsstand sales have a much lower percentage of circulation on campus than those that are financed by a compulsory student activity fee or are subsidized. In the latter case, the press run usually is better than 90 percent of the enrollment. Fifty papers may be dropped at the Sigma Chi house under the free circulation program. But on campuses where the reader must subscribe, the house may have only five to ten subscriptions. While financial independence through subscriptions frees the newspaper from a variety of pressures, the counter argument is that the newspaper that has a 2,500 circulation on a campus of 10,000 would be inadequately fulfilling its obligations to the community.

Nevertheless, the question of whether students, and the university, should be forced to finance a publication with which they disagree and over which they have little control is being asked with increasing frequency as the editors become involved with issues deeper than the retention of the basketball coach and the selection of the student body president.

For many years, college newsmen said their schools had an obligation to support them so long as they published a diversity of opinion on their editorial page, kept their letters column open to all, and covered campus activities.

They are less sure nowadays that they want to lean on their administrations and student politicians for help through subsidies and the compulsory student fee. This could compromise their freedom, they believe. A poll of student editors I took in 1968 disclosed that 30 percent of them listed "independence from the college" as one of their most important goals.

It is easier to talk about the condition of independence than to bring it off. The UCLA *Daily Bruin* has received a subsidy of about $60,000 a year, which would be difficult but not impossible to replace with increased advertising. But Brian Weiss, a former editor, had a question:

"Would the University 'support' such an independent publication by not putting into competition with it an 'official' school paper, which would inevitably attract the bulk of national advertising?"

Joseph R. Bankoff, a former editor-in-chief of the *Exponent* at Purdue University, states the case for the financially independent newspaper:

The student newspaper should operate on as realistic a financial basis as possible. Realizing the pitfalls and the limitations involved both in terms of student time and revenue availability, yet I would point to the educational experience derived from student management and financial responsibility for their own efforts.

Put rather simply, if the revenue comes from the university, the paper's voice must call out the university "line"; if the revenue comes from the student fees, then it must reflect the views and serve the needs of theoretically all the students, but at least the majority of the students; but if the revenue is earned by the newspaper as an entity in itself, then the paper is required to be nothing more than the articulate voice of its own staff operating in a purely competitive market for personnel and ideas.

Since the discovery of the affluent college-age market by business, advertising income has increased substantially. Over the next few years it appears probable that the *Yale Daily News, Harvard Crimson,* and the few other independent college newspapers will be joined by others—but only in prime market areas.

Most student journalists seek financial independence, and most administrators would be pleased, too. But this is not feasible on most campuses. Alternative plans always involve some kind of subsidy, and a subsidy requires suspension of the desire to control the expenditure of the funds. This can be accomplished by the university's allocating a single sum to a publications board, which then budgets the appropriation to the various campus publications. Another plan involves a contract between newspaper and university whereby the university grants an amount in return for a campus newspaper. The terms of the contract protect the staff from capricious administrative decisions, and a publications board hears charges by either party of contract violations.

Every administrator complains that the student newspaper refuses to publish much of the information he considers essential for the proper functioning of the enterprise. In the surveys I have made of the student press, it is clear that students and administrators have very different views of the functions of the student press. Whereas the administrator ranks high the dissemination of information about the school, the editor considers this one of his lesser responsibilities.

In the press for space, which is always a problem for the editor, the news about meetings, class changes, and the like are compressed or dropped.

There is no question that many editors ignore legitimate campus news. But rather than rely on the possibility such news will be published, administrators have sought other, more certain means.

Some financial arrangements involve the university in a special advertising contract with the student newspaper, which gives the administration a specific amount of space for news and notices it deems important but which it realizes the newspaper will not, or cannot, publish as news.

On many campuses, supplementary university publications have been published—newsletters, monthly magazines, mailings, etc. Of course, the readership is not as great as it would be were the information to be carried in the newspaper. One device used by some administrations is the stuffed supplement. Many of the newspaper's financial problems would be solved were the administration to buy space in the campus newspaper at generous advertising rates.

Summary

No formal arrangement between the administrator and the student journalist will work unless the administrator is willing to consider the newspaper an educational project, guaranteeing the student journalist the same freedom to pursue truth as is granted all students.

What position can a man of reason maintain toward the college press? He can take to it essentially the same attitude he takes toward any other educational enterprise on the campus: the desire to assist through moral and financial means the education of the student.

The man of conscience knows the risks yet encourages the development of an open campus. He seeks out the teachers and students who will provoke the play of ideas, for he knows that they extend the frontiers of knowledge. If he is pragmatic, he knows the time is past when he can control the thoughts and the activities of the young. Should he try to censor them, whether they are in the psychology laboratory or the newsroom, he assists in the destruction of the university.

Schools and campus newspapers have sought to set up systems whereby the school is guaranteed comprehensive and fair coverage of campus activities and the newspaper's freedom is inviolate. No arrangement I know of has been discovered that removes the tension between the two.

The independently financed, separately incorporated college newspaper comes close to avoiding the painful confrontations that lead to administrative or student excesses. The newspaper is free, and the school can demonstrate to its on- and off-campus constituencies that it has no control over the newspaper.

These newspapers usually have a tradition of mature journalism. Free from the feeling that they are constantly under the scrutiny of their paymaster, these young journalists go at their job of practicing independent journalism.

The newspaper may well antagonize its sources. At Harvard, President Pusey has remarked that the *Crimson* causes him unrest, and the *Crimson* with its off-campus plant and complete financial independence is probably the ideal college-newspaper relationship.

Few newspapers have the economic resources and the tradition of the *Crimson*. But many large, well-financed universities can make arrangements with their campus newspapers that will keep confrontations to a minimum.

The newspaper's financial support should come from the student activity fee rather than a school subsidy. When the university pays the bills, legislators, donors, and alumni can legitimately question the expenditure of general funds. Students can complain of the use of their money on the newspaper, too. But on the several campuses where this has occurred, the complaints rarely generate large-scale student support.

The arrangement usually calls for a student group, often elected, to appropriate the activity fee among the many student groups: clubs, student government, tutoring organizations, the several publications, and a myriad other activities.

The appropriation would be made following presentation to the student financial group by the publications board. The creation of a board is essential. It would have major responsibility for hearing complaints against the staff, in addition to its other activities. The board is the buffer between the newspaper and the institution and on a number of campuses has provided the president with a defensive weapon to hold off the critics who seek immediate action against the newspaper.

V John B. Wood
College Newspapers — Northeast

I have made exhaustive (or cursory) studies of the newspapers at Harvard, Yale, (Princeton), Dartmouth, Cornell, University of Pennsylvania, (Brown), Columbia, Boston University, Wesleyan, (Williams), (Amherst), Tufts, (Brandeis), (Duke), (University of Massachusetts), (University of Southern Connecticut), and Vassar. Here are some tentative conclusions.

All these papers are written and edited by undergraduates. There is no overt censorship, no prior readership of copy. All are in theory editorially independent; some papers have review boards, consisting of students, past editors, faculty, administration, and occasionally local businessmen, but these boards act only after the fact. Their power is limited and generally unrealized.

In practice, however, the independence of these papers is undermined continually by the universities they serve. Many faculty and administration members say they would like to "improve" their campus paper, to help it present a "fairer" picture of the university. This concern is generally based on a fear that undergraduate journalism will misuse a privileged position on campus to misrepresent the university to the outside world. The papers at larger universities are better able to preserve their independence, but all are subject to some form of encroachment. The specific areas of contention seem to be these:

1. *Financial dependence*— Most Ivy League papers (Harvard, Yale, Princeton, Dartmouth, Cornell, Columbia) are financially independent, supporting themselves entirely through advertising and circulation revenue. Others receive funds in lieu of subscription, either from the administration or from a student activities fund; the paper is then circulated free. This subsidy invariably provokes the question of editorial independence; the papers at Penn, BU, and Tufts have recently renounced their subsidies because of alleged attempts at censorship. Other, generally smaller papers operate with a stipend from the college and do not feel themselves compromised (Wesleyan, Amherst, Vassar).

2. *Other direct university sanctions*— The less autonomous papers also

John B. Wood, Managing Editor, *Yale Daily News.*

feel threatened by the possibility of a variety of other direct university sanctions. The *News* at Boston University expects to be evicted from its university-owned office. The editors of the Columbia *Spectator* were threatened with expulsion for "conduct unbecoming to a Columbia student" after siding with radical students in the disturbances there. The trustees of the Cornell *Sun* advised the editors that dependence on the campus mail for circulation "would make the paper doubly or triply vulnerable for the University in the event of retributions." These dangers seem more imagined than real; no administration is likely to attempt overt suppression of free press.

3. *The university as a news source*— College papers rely on administration sources for much of their news. Although two papers (BU, Cornell) recently called for the resignation of their university presidents, most are careful to maintain cordial relations with administration personnel. The papers at Harvard, Yale, and Cornell have been embarrassed recently by major campus stories appearing first in the *New York Times* due to inexplicable oversights by university officials or news bureaus. The recurrent problem of inside information—when may "off-the-record" remarks be published?—is aggravated by the tightness of the university community and is handled differently by virtually all of the papers.

4. *Election*— The election or selection of editors necessarily affects a college paper's policies. Papers whose officers are elected by the student body at large, by a student publications committee, or by a faculty-influenced board of directors are likely to be less than critical of these groups. Most Ivy League editors are elected by their staffs, but even here the precise make-up of the electorate is important: Do senior editors vote? Do business personnel vote on editorial positions? Vice versa? The effect on election of editors and hence policy is more direct than might be expected. At Yale this year, aspiring juniors forewent election of editors and resolved to rule by committee; anarchy ensued.

5. *The college paper as representative of the student body*— This is a quasi-philosophical issue with immediate effect on editorial content. Some college administrations and student government groups wish their campus papers were more "representative"—i.e., carried more campus news, printed faculty notices, or took a more "moderate" editorial policy. At Tufts and Penn, a fixed percentage of campus news was suggested as a prerequisite for financial support. Most editors reject this concept of "representative journalism," insisting they are responsible only to higher journalistic ideals:

"Most students want to get through here in four years without thinking too much. We try to prod them a bit." —George LeMaitre, Dartmouth.

"Our responsibility is to present the news objectively and our opinions convincingly. No more." —Stuart Madden, Penn.

"We are representative only in that we are students. We do not pretend to be objective; we are responsible finally to our own observations and opinions." —Steve Davis, Boston University.

"I don't think we have any delusions about leading the student body; our job is to give them as much that is true as we can, and not to lie editorially." —James Fallows, Harvard.

In practice, most papers define their position politically to the left of whatever student opinion seems prevalent and to the right of the radical action groups.

6. *Transition*— A fundamental conflict exists between student editors, who glimpse their universities for four years, and college administrators, whose stake in their institutions may last a lifetime. Past editors at Harvard, Penn, Columbia, and Tufts remarked on the impatience with gradual change common to Young Turks of college journalism. To minimize the editorial schizophrenia often caused by the ascension of junior editors, some papers provide for a "transitional" steering committee. At Cornell, senior editors remain on the paper's governing board six months after their active terms expire; at Penn, underclassmen are allowed to compete for secondary editorial positions in preparation for election as editors in senior year. "We encourage the newly elected editors to feel their position and responsibility in the University, and to think constructively rather than destructively in the first months of their term." —Duncan M. McIntyre, faculty stockholder of the *Cornell Daily Sun*.

Some Factual Background

The Harvard Crimson— Daily except Sunday, undergraduate, self-supported on advertising and subscriptions totaling $150,000. Circulation: 5,000. Staff: 75, divided among news, editorial, photo, and business boards. Executive board of ten senior editors is the final authority. Editorial policies are voted on by all news and editorial personnel, usually about thirty. Editors are "nominated" by the retiring board and "ratified" by the entire paper.

No faculty or administration adviser. Biweekly press conferences with President Pusey are on the record.

The Yale Daily News— Daily except Saturday and Sunday, undergraduate, self-supported on a budget of $180,000. Circulation: 4,500. Staff: 120, divided among news, business, and photo boards. Managing board of eight senior editors has final say in editorial and business matters. Editorial policies determined by the editor "in consultation with" other senior editors. Dissenting, signed editorials common this year, as at the

34 THE STUDENT NEWSPAPER

Crimson. Editors are elected by the junior staff and the senior managing board; a majority is required for the three top positions.

No faculty or administration adviser. Unscheduled interviews with President Brewster have been on the record this year after a history of "misunderstandings."

The Dartmouth— Daily except Saturday and Sunday, undergraduate, self-supported on a budget of $80,000. Circulation: 3,700. Office is leased permanently from the university. Staff: 40. Board of proprietors has eight students, one alumnus, one faculty member, one administration member; meets three times a year. Editorial policies determined solely by the editor. A summary of national news appears on page 1 every day, with never more than two nonuniversity stories on a page. Editors are appointed by the retiring board.

Little communication with retiring college president. Conferences with the college dean have frequently included "background" material. "Many of the more radical papers find us establishment."

The Daily Pennsylvanian— Daily except Sunday, undergraduate. In 1967, the *DP* received $18,000 from the Student Government to cover student subscriptions; the paper was distributed free. In 1968, after a dispute with the UPSG, the paper received no funds and supported itself on advertising alone, with a budget of $100,000. In 1969, the *DP* received $12,000 from the university to cover faculty and administration subscriptions and $18,000 from the newly formed student association. Until 1969, the popularly elected Student Publications Committee had final authority and could have suspended *DP* editors. Currently, an advisory committee of faculty, administration, and non-*DP* students is being formed; their recommendations may be overruled by vote of the *Daily Pennsylvanian* staff. Editors are appointed by the retiring board; editorials are voted on by the entire staff.

No scheduled press conferences with President Harnwell. *DP* may submit questions in writing to be answered at a press conference by Harnwell's aides. *DP* has called for Harnwell's resignation.

A bright and innovative paper. Page 1 contains a column of campus news briefs and one in-depth feature daily, à la the *Christian Science Monitor*.

The Cornell Daily Sun— Daily except Saturday and Sunday, undergraduate, self-supported on advertising and subscriptions totaling $160,000. Circulation: 18,000 tabloid. Staff: 60 full time, approximately 40 part time. Board of directors, who hold preferred stock in this corporation (most other papers are organized as partnerships), includes senior editors and must include one faculty member, one administration member, and one local businessman. Editors are elected by their own class (i.e., juniors) on the *Sun*. Editorial policy determined by an editorial committee of about six.

The News at Boston University— Weekly, undergraduate. In 1967, the *BU News* was given $50,000, which was taken out in tuition by the senior editors, to cover free subscriptions. In 1969, the administration pays $10,000 for faculty subscriptions; other copies are sold at newsstands. Circulation: approximately 17,000. Staff: 40. Editors are elected by the entire *News* board. In 1967, faculty and administration were 40 percent of the governing Publications Committee; now there are no faculty advisers and no nonstudents on the *News* board. Editors claim 4,000 of the 17,000 copies of the infamous "Sex" issue were stolen off the newsstands by administration. "Administration members give *News* reporters no special consideration over outside media."

Tufts Observer— Weekly, undergraduate, replaced the "more arty" *Tufts Weekly* this year. Receives $16,000 (50 percent of budget) from Student Activities Committee to cover free subscriptions. Staff: 20. *Observer* hopes to end subsidy next year with election of radical editor. Editors are elected by the staff with the approval of the Publications Committee, a student group. No censorship or faculty adviser.

Wesleyan Argus— Biweekly, undergraduate. College Body Committee contributes $18,000 (30 percent of budget) to cover free subscriptions. Circulation: 2,100. Staff: 15. Editorial policies at the discretion of the editor; seniors appoint the succeeding editors. No faculty or administration adviser. Rarely speak with college president, most news comes from the University News Bureau.

VI
William Porter

What Should Be the Role of a Student Newspaper?

Most journalism professors are to some extent knowledgeable about student publications, even if they'd prefer not to be. The observations which follow represent my own experience, my observations, and the more salient agonies of my colleagues across the country.

Practically all student newspapers today are set up within one of three different structures. The first of these is the rarest and in a sense the most "efficient," if efficiency is to be measured in terms of minimum trauma.

1. The system is one in which full-time professionals occupy the key positions of the newspaper. In the University of Missouri's School of Journalism, as I understand it, the *Missourian*'s editor is a student, but the managing editor is a faculty member (and, of course, an experienced newsman). Other key decision-making personnel are faculty members. There is relatively little chance for student lapses in judgment, taste, or respect for elders to get into print. It is important to observe that the student in this situation is not dealing with a cold-eyed city editor who almost incidentally will also give him a grade. Although I'm sure that Missouri faculty could give lots of examples of difficulties, comparatively speaking there is little sedition raised in the *Missourian*. Furthermore, it is an excellent small-town daily, although not as good as the *Ann Arbor News*, which it rather resembles. It is commonly said in Columbia that many readers of the paper do not even know that it is published by the university.

The second category is at the other end of the permissive spectrum, and I would include in this group the organizational pattern of which the *Michigan Daily* is a part.

2. Under the system, the paper is under control of a board of directors which in theory directs its operations. In practice, the student staff has no direct supervision. The only form of "control" is the suspension or removal of student staff members. Whatever their particular make-up, these directing boards are always reluctant to take such drastic action.

Most of the student papers in this category were once completely off

William Porter, Chairman, Journalism Department, University of Michigan.

campus, produced privately and generally for profit by groups of self-selected students. They have moved into the vague university relationship signified by the elected board and nonprofit status in part because of the increasing need for subsidy and in part because of the wistful administrative delusion that getting them a little closer to the university will make them a little more responsible.

The *Harvard Crimson,* the Cornell *Sun,* the *Daily Illini,* the Columbia *Spectator,* etc., are all of this pattern. This includes almost all of what are generally conceded to be the best college papers in the country.

I feel that both experience and good sense indicate that this is the best framework for student publications.

I think the chief advantage of such a scheme can be summed up simply: an institution's chance of having a student paper which will accurately reflect its intellectual dimensions and educational purposes are far better under this system than any other. The more elaborate and pervasive the system of control from outside, the more docilely pedestrian the kids who'll want to work on the paper.

The best case to be made for this system, however, is rather like Winston Churchill's defense of democracy: all the other systems are so much worse. The worst of all is the following, the one in the middle.

3. This system is built around a central role which does not really exist in the other systems: that of "adviser." Advisers, under this system, may take many forms—sometimes they are called "publishers"—but the system is always marked by roughly the same mode of operation. The adviser is always around while the paper is in preparation; there is a fervent hope that he will be consulted upon all controversial issues, and his advice accepted. Sometimes he simply sits in his office, busily shuffling papers while waiting to be consulted, wondering What They're Up To Now (Indiana uses this system); sometimes he stays home, but he's on call, rather like a medical resident (Iowa was using this system during my last years there). He is almost invariably a low-ranking member of the department of journalism and a part-time employee of the board of publications.

There is seldom a clear definition of what the adviser's powers are in this situation; he is generally reluctant to act like a censor, although in times of crisis he tends to become one in self-protection. The system is marked by such crises almost at regular intervals, in which the adviser finally clothes himself in the awful majesty of the board and the university and says no. The young scream foul and point out that under whatever code presumably governs the system the adviser does not have such authority. Eventually the tumult dies, and the adviser goes back to his regular routine of post hoc analysis; the staff meets for an hour early in the afternoon, and he goes over the sins of the previous day.

There are two amiable pretenses in this system: the first is that the adviser is really exercising a teaching function, not censorship, and the second is that the paper really is free. The load of hypocrisy under these conditions is simply too great for a man of intelligence and sensitivity to carry for very long.

The flaws in this adviser-centered system are numerous. For twenty years I taught in the school of journalism at a university which not only had an "adviser" but also a "publisher" for the student daily, and I have seen it operate at firsthand. I make the assertions which follow without much documentation, because of space, but I can provide however much evidence might be required.

First, the capacity of the student paper for "causing trouble" is in no way diminished. The duller students take the official word at face value, assume that the paper is indeed free, and plunge ahead with frequently embarrassing results; the bright ones know that it is not and set out to prove it, with disastrous ones. The adviser system proves to be no control at all 99 percent of the time; its chiefly discernible function is the development of cynicism in the minds of students and—if the adviser gets a great deal of pressure himself, which is generally the case—faculty. The system sometimes seems to work because a long tradition of authoritarianism has made it certain that alert and enterprising students wouldn't be caught dead working on the paper. But the adviser system never works the way it is supposed to work.

The reason is simply that the role is impossible. This can be demonstrated in a hypothetical case. Let's say that a reporter on the student daily has come upon evidence that the school has in the past covertly trained CIA agents (just to provide a wildly improbable example). The adviser gets wind of this; he checks with the university administration (a process, incidentally, which does not exactly enhance his own dignity) and discovers that the story is to be squelched. Now then: at what point shall he start "advising," and what advice shall he give?

Should he nip it in the bud by telling the reporter that it's really not worth following up? (Impossible! He's a journalism professor, and a man can lie only so much; it's a terrific story.) Or should he simply indicate that the kid can go ahead if he wants to but that it's highly improbable that it will come to anything? (This will not offend his professional conscience quite so much, but neither will it stop the young reporter if he's any good.)

Let's say the reporter goes ahead and the adviser learns that the story, or its first installment, has been written. Is this, perhaps, the place where he should move? Should he demand to see the story, search it frantically until he finds something inaccurate, and forbid the whole story on those tenuous grounds? Supposing the student indicates his willingness to correct the inaccuracy but insists on proceeding?

This hypothetical case could be strung out indefinitely without ever finding a spot where an adviser, exercising an honest advisory function, can sidetrack that embarrassing story. If he is a man with any self-respect, he can do one of two things: He can say to the reporter, "That's a good story, and I'll back you." Or he can say, "I'm going to kill this story, and I'm going to kill it because my bosses feel that it's not in the best interests of the institution." Neither of these courses would seem to be "advising."

Various child psychologists are said to approve spanking, not because of its value in disciplining the child, but because it's good therapy for the parents. It has often occurred to me that the chief value of the poor devils who advise college papers is that they are paid employees who provide a handy target for tongue-lashings.

I once knew a young professor who felt that the university at which we both were then employed should encourage hostility in the school newspaper; he proposed in an AAUP meeting that the university give an award to the most controversial story of the year (he has since become a dean at another institution and, oddly enough, no longer espouses this cause at all). Most of us are different; most journalism teachers, including this writer, can well understand the concern for getting on with the main business of the university which finds the arrogant animus of student editors irritating. Nobody likes to be bugged; only a masochist could smile cheerfully while being slandered and ask for more. But two things still need to be said.

First, there is absolutely no evidence that the adviser, or semicontrol, system produces more institutional equanimity. The authorities of such institutions as Iowa or Indiana or Oregon are bugged just as vigorously, and as often, as those of Michigan, particularly when one takes into consideration the make-up of the respective student bodies.

Second, one small reminder of a sentiment set out earlier: the present system here, as in most of the other great institutions in this country, is the one which most accurately and honestly reflects the long-range quality and objectives of the institution. It is very easy to say this from a distance, with one's own ox ungored; the hard part is to believe it when brash youths are trying to take the place apart as if it were an old Erector set. But a good many of the things which make the University of Michigan what it is are inconvenient, and painful, and expensive.

We put up with them, I suppose, because we know that these are the things that have made the place great.

VII Arthur E. Sutton
A Few Thoughts on the Use of Obscenity by Campus Journalists

The word f - - - is our most common expletive to express violent hostility. I do not think this is by accident. —Rollo May [1]

Today, many of the young (or would-be young) use sexual display or obscene language quite deliberately as shock weapons of protest against "the Establishment." —Time [2]

For a variety of reasons, some as yet ill-defined, many young people are increasingly hostile—contemptuous might be more accurate—to the present social order in America, the values esteemed by the ruling generation, and the consequential socioeconomic and political decision-making flowing from such conventional wisdom and beliefs.

In their search for a way to adequately express their dissatisfaction, young avant-garde leaders—who are, inevitably, the brightest and most perceptively sensitive of their generation and are thus more likely to cluster on the better college and university campuses—have seized on obscenity as an effective way to show displeasure with society and, at the same time, publicly proclaim their commitment to a new social order, one with a new set of priorities, that makes a complete break with things as they are. As such, it is a choice that reflects both childishness—outrage for outrage sake —and idealism—the quest for a utopian society free from greed, violence, hypocrisy and selfishness.

The young avant-garde leaders wish to capture the attention of the ruling generation. They wish to be taken seriously. Their goal is nothing short of a revolution in the present social, economic, and political life of the United States. They are restless, idealistic, dissatisfied, and angry.

In this context, the selection of obscenity to capture attention and express commitment to new values is a natural and, indeed, quite logical one. If

---
Arthur E. Sutton, Special Assistant to the Chancellor, University of California, Riverside.
1. *Love and Will* (New York: W. W. Norton & Co., 1969).
2. "The Sex Explosion," 11 July 1969.

one wishes to utterly outrage the middle-class, middle-aged mind in America, one could scarcely do better than to use the word *f* – – – and its numerous derivatives on every possible occasion. Additionally, the use of obscenity establishes a distinct image in the media that effectively breaks with the past while providing distinctive identification for adherents and followers. Eldridge Cleaver is but one example of this technique.

So much for why obscenity has come to be the trademark of many in today's militant, with-it generation. What are the options available for dealing with this problem as it affects campus journalism?

One could, of course, use the methods of repression and censorship. The words could be banned, and copies of newspapers ignoring the ban could be seized and destroyed. Such a response to the politics of obscenity would come to student militants as nothing short of an answer to prayer. It would carry all the attention-getting and commercial benefits that accrued to books and plays able to acquire a "banned in Boston" label in an earlier age.

One could ignore the problem and hope that, in time, it would go away. This might be a possible solution to a privately supported college or university, but it is politically unrealistic as a policy for the University of California at this time.

The third alternative, and quite obviously the one I favor, is to discuss the problem frankly with student journalists from the various campuses of the university.

The setting is less important than the manner in which the problem is presented and the attitude of those making the presentation toward the use of obscenity as a form of social protest. If the approach to the problem reflects outrage or shock or extreme disapproval, then the university leadership is immediately placed on the defensive and the session will disintegrate into a debate between the students and the administrative or faculty spokesmen. This will only serve to reinforce the determination of the students to continue, if not escalate, their use of obscenity in the pages of their respective newspapers. In such a case, the attempted cure would have served but to intensify the disease.

In my opinion, student journalists should be frankly told the practical effects of a continuation of the use of obscenity by their newspapers. It is clearly counterproductive to the goals of the new or revised social order they profess to support.

There is obviously a great deal wrong with our society today. We cannot continue much longer to give preference to the unblack, the unyoung, and the unpoor without creating some severe dislocations in our national life. We must face the problems of environmental pollution, urban decay, marijuana and drug usage among the young, unjust taxation, and racial unrest and violence and begin to develop appropriate solutions. It is time for action. We've talked enough. Campus newspapers have an important role to play in making such action possible.

The energy and idealism, as well as the essential creativity, necessary to develop these solutions is the finest contribution our young people can make to the urgent process of implementing constructive social change. But to implement such change requires the understanding and support of the ruling generation and the institutions they control. Controlled change, without violent revolution, requires the teamwork of both young and old.

Student journalists need to be told that the use of obscenity makes such understanding and support, such teamwork between the generations, at best difficult, at worst impossible. They should be asked to examine their own personal commitments: Is the goal to shock? To outrage? To provoke? Or is it to advance ideas for change and create a climate in which such ideas can find eventual acceptance by the leadership of the larger community beyond the campus?

Admittedly, for a small percentage of students, the goal is to shock, to invite repression, to provoke anger. For these few, American society is totally without redeeming qualities, and the sooner it is destroyed, the better.

For the vast majority of committed students, there is recognition of the need for continuity in a time of change, there is understanding that a society that attempts to deny its past has no future. It is in this group that most, if not all, our campus journalists are to be found.

The problem of obscenity in campus culture is a present and growing one. Unless it is handled with skill and considerable finesse, it can easily become the torch destroying the academic freedom on which the life of any great college or university depends. One thing is certain: it cannot continue to be ignored at the University of California. Not here. Not now.

VIII
John E. Moore

Reflections on Campus Press Problems

These reflections on problems confronting the campus newspapers and possible responses to them are not entirely random, but neither are they as well ordered as I would like.

Money

1. Dependence upon Associated Students' appropriations leaves the newspaper vulnerable to reprisals from student government, either because it has been critical of student government (which is frequently desirable) or because student government is vaguely dissatisfied with the quality of the newspaper. In either case, it is remarkable how similarly some members of student government and some members of the Board of Regents respond —by proposing to cut or eliminate funds.

Where reduced appropriations reflect a reordering of student priorities rather than some form of reprisal, the first items to get cut relate to attendance at conferences, salaries, and similar "trimmings." I would guess that many of the proposals discussed at our meeting in Berkeley—including visits by distinguished journalists or William Arthur's proposed seminars— would not be funded by student government.

2. Dependence upon the Associated Students, which on our campus does not include graduate student representation, frees graduate students of payment for a newspaper which most of them read and deprives them of representation on both the editorial staff and the Communications Board. A direct subsidy drawn from both undergraduate and graduate student fees might resolve many of these problems.

Obscenity and Ideological Bias

I agree with Art Sutton (part VII) that obscenity divorced from reporting (e.g., a speech by Eldridge Cleaver) often reflects an immature form of social protest. I am disinclined to characterize an entire student body as

---
John E. Moore, Faculty Representative, University of California, Santa Barbara, Communications Board.

43

immature, just as I am disinclined to assume that all students are radicals. But I do believe that there are significant differences between the values of members of the Board of Regents and the college-age population, just as there appear to be significant differences between the values of college-age youth on and off the campuses (see, for example, the recent CBS series on the generation gap).

What I am trying to say is that the standards to be applied in evaluating our campus newspapers should give greater weight to the values of the students who compose their principal clientele than to the values of the Board of Regents. I would ask if a student newspaper reflects the diverse interests and values of the student body with reasonable accuracy and if it aspires to professional standards of journalism in distinguishing between reporting and editorializing. If the answer to both of these questions is yes, I would waste no time condemning student values with which I disagree but proceed to ask what steps might be taken to enable student editors to implement those professional standards to which they aspire.

Reforms

The following are listed in descending order of feasibility.

1. Rely more heavily on the Communications Board for friendly criticism. At present, too much of the board's time is devoted to mickey-mouse budgetary transfers. In light of a recent effort to reconstitute and revitalize the board, I am more than ever impressed with the self-perpetuating tendency of this preoccupation with trivia (which I regret to say I have done little to arrest). Because it is often dealing with petty issues, many of the board's members do not take its work seriously; because they do not take its work seriously, the board continues to concentrate on petty issues; etc. A vigorous chairman might be able to break this vicious circle, but he would risk the displeasure of his peers in departing from traditional norms. Perhaps the personal costs of attempting to transform the board's mission could be reduced by linking the change with a well-publicized monthly meeting at which the board would hear complaints about the various media. Individual members would thus be relieved of playing the role of perennial critics. Any such effort to rely more extensively on the board itself would have to be accompanied by such mundane reforms as regularized meetings.

2. Adopt the Commission's proposal for annual or semiannual seminars involving the editors from all nine campuses.

3. Following UCLA's example, encourage monthly seminars for staff

members on each of the campuses to hear distinguished practitioners or professors of journalism. (Encouragement consists mainly of providing funds.)

4. Institute a journalism class for which all participants would receive credit, with provision for additional "independent studies" credit for members of the newspaper staff. Apart from its emphasis on professional standards, such a class would provide much-needed compensation for students who are asked to devote a substantial amount of time to producing a newspaper. Without incentives in the form of credit or money, it is no wonder that cliques develop—editors quite naturally look to their friends for help. If English departments are reluctant to sponsor such a class, perhaps speech departments would be more willing.

5. Since I was the only straight academician present at the Berkeley meeting, I am understandably less skeptical than my fellows regarding the ability of a well-chosen faculty member to provide dispassionate advice. As I reflect on the difficulty of securing a counterpart to UCLA's technical adviser on the smaller campuses (which also lack a school of journalism to shelter him), I am increasingly attracted by the possibility of locating someone with credentials in both journalism and academia. For example, several of my colleagues in political science could think of former journalists who were presently teaching—or were qualified to teach—in academic departments. These are probably rare birds, and few departments could afford to shelter them in a regular position. But if the regents were willing to cover the entire cost of a fifty-fifty arrangement (teaching and publications advice), such departments as political science, history, or speech might be prepared to undertake a diligent search. With the suggested subsidy, these departments could afford to be flexible in adjusting teaching loads in response to demand for performance of advisory functions. This is a risky business, since it depends upon both faculty confidence in the instructor and student confidence in the adviser, but I believe the students would view an academic umbrella with less suspicion than an administrative location, such as a public information office.

Parting Thoughts

If student newspapers perform an important function, which I believe they do, no useful purpose will be served by driving them underground, either by cutting off funds or increasing regental surveillance. And whatever the official relationship between the regents and the campus newspapers, the regents are going to feel the heat of public opinion, if not legal actions. An angry citizen does not take time to ascertain who is officially responsible for an offensive article and probably wouldn't care much if the regents were able to disclaim legal responsibility. The conclusion I reach from the foregoing premises is that the regents should try to avoid the trap into which student government so frequently falls—responding to a meritorious but faltering enterprise by reducing support, when the principal hope for improvement lies with increased support.

IX
The Commission's Recommendations

The Commission must emphasize at the outset that there is no ideal "solution" for the problems of the campus press.

Across the country there are abundant examples of student newspapers that have led the way in exposing evils and achieving improvements on campus and in communities. There are also plentiful examples of ineptness, unfairness, and other excesses. The one is the price of the other—just as in journalism at large.

In general and with occasional exceptions, the most effective, constructive, and responsible student newspapers across the country have been those with a strong tradition of independence and editorial freedom. The process, however, inevitably involves tensions and give and take.

It is not possible for a Commission like this one to lay down precise formulae for all campuses. It can only hope to suggest guidelines that may keep the tensions within reason and help campus journalism to be of greater service and significance.

Number 1

It is the Commission's view that many of the concerns, disagreements, and exchanges of accusations within the University of California system and its student publications flow from an erroneous premise.

That premise is that student publications necessarily constitute a form of official publication for which university administrators bear inherent responsibility.

The Commission challenges this widely held view, holding it a misconception resulting from the pervasive and abrasive nature of the communications process itself.

The reporting of events and of statement and opinion is one of the seedbeds of American thought. Out of the cross-pollinization of controversial opinion has come the growth of Western civilization. The process begins naturally in the academic world, and to inhibit the questioning and probing of student journalists by the burden of official imprimatur is both unrealistic and counterproductive to the constantly proclaimed academic thrust for unfettered intellectual challenge.

Admittedly, student journalism differs from other forms of student activity in its public exposure and the financial requirements for publication. Nevertheless, the Commission has concluded that student journalism is a valid campus activity akin to all other forms of voluntary student participation.

This does not imply that student journalism should operate without responsibility or guidance. The Commission is convinced responsibility can be achieved and guidance provided by means other than official university direction.

It is the Commission's first and basic recommendation that it be accepted and made repeatedly clear by all concerned—regents, administrators, and campus newspaper staffs—that these newspapers are not "official" organs of the university.

This should be stressed in a standing statement in each paper's masthead, and the university's officials should take formal action stating explicitly not only that student publications are not vested with official status but that none may be labeled in any manner as to indicate such official approval.

Number 2

The Commission believes that the experiences of nonofficial, self-financed student publications at institutions like Cornell, Dartmouth, Harvard, Michigan, and Yale (among others) have produced convincing evidence that responsibility, service to student bodies, and self-esteem of newspaper staffs generally result from fiscal independence.

Giving representative students full responsibility has usually resulted in sounder news coverage by student staffs, more thoughtful expression of viewpoints, and closer attention to the expressed needs of student and faculty subscribers. Alumni directors often provide fiscal stability and continuity.

Further, the reports which have been examined indicate that such independent campus newspapers attract more volunteer staff members. The Commission notes in this regard that one of the major problems on many of the University of California campuses has been the lack of adequate staffing.

The 1968–69 University of California financing pattern is shown in the table on page 49.

Commission discussions with student editors disclosed that only the Berkeley, Los Angeles, and Santa Barbara campus staffs envisage the possibility of those publications becoming self-supporting in the near future. The editors of the Berkeley and Los Angeles campus newspapers advanced

THE COMMISSION'S RECOMMENDATIONS   49

the opinion this goal could be achieved if these operations were given a five-year period in which the necessary adjustments could be accomplished without severe strain. The other campus editors (other than the three mentioned) did not believe such a transition readily possible under present circumstances.

UNIVERSITY OF CALIFORNIA STUDENT NEWSPAPER FINANCES, 1968–69

CAMPUS	TOTAL EXPENSES	ASUC SUBSIDY	PERCENTAGE OF TOTAL
Berkeley	$226,400	$42,000	18.5
Davis	51,270	20,270	39.5
Irvine*	20,317	13,117	64.6
Los Angeles	228,425	64,175	28.1
Riverside	14,215	5,464	31.4
San Diego*	15,795	5,445	34.5
Santa Barbara	85,683	23,336	27.0
Santa Cruz	5,900	1,900	33.2

Note: Medical Center figures not provided.
* 1969–70 budget figures.

For the *Daily Californian* and the *Bruin*, the Commission recommends immediate feasibility studies—the drawing up of firm plans for evolution to self-financing status. Such studies should evaluate budgets, advertising and subscription rates, and the amount of ASUC payments from student fees for the period ranging from full subsidy to full self-support. These feasibility studies might provide a model for the other campus journals at some later time.[1]

For these other campus publications, the Commission recommends that the financing through student fees be established with the ASUC by contract agreements before each school year and that similar contract terms also be arranged with university administrations for the delivery of such papers as are required. Contract agreements seem desirable in view of the episodes of threats voiced against student editors by some campus dissenters and administrators. There was reported to the Commission one open instance of an ASUC group cutting the campus newspaper's budget and

1. At one point during the Commission's deliberations, Mr. Isaacs advanced the belief that there was a "luxury" factor built into the two major campus publications—the inserting of the special entertainment-cultural sections, "Weekly Magazine" in the *Daily Californian* and "Intro" in the *Daily Bruin*. He suggested that these special sections be removed as inserts and offered for sale separately to those desiring this type of coverage. The three other commissioners disagreed, and after further reflection Mr. Isaacs withdrew his proposal, stating that the projected feasibility studies should make it evident to the campus staffs whether these sections should be continued as free inserts.

then offering the sum back in return for its own regular column—a despicable form of campus political blackmail.

In these cases of publication's being assured through contract fees, the Commission recommends that basic authority be vested in boards of publications. The Commission urges flexibility in the pattern to assure campus newspapers of reasonable representation of the communities served. Where campuses contain both undergraduate and graduate student bodies, the make-up of the publications boards should be roughly proportionate in size to the student bodies. This should be subject to annual review of enrollment figures, and the formula should allow for increase and decrease to reflect these changes.

It is the Commission's view that those members of a publications board representing the student population should come from the standard, accepted organizations which operate in normal legislative patterns.[2]

These publications boards should provide student editors with insulation from both the pressures of campus politics and of administrations.

The function of such publications boards should be one of active publisher —assuming responsibility, directing editors, and otherwise accepting the duties falling on any publisher.

Occasional meetings of such boards are insufficient. There should be regular meetings, and there should be a continuing critique of the newspapers' performance by such boards.

Number 3

In California, as elsewhere, student editors are sometimes confused as to their paper's role. Some are tempted to accept as their model a *Berkeley Barb* or other so-called underground paper. It is the Commission's view that the role and obligation of a supplementary journal is quite different from that of a principal journal, which is *the* community (or campus) newspaper.

A supplementary publication can justifiably be as causist or as unbalanced as it wishes. The principal newspaper of a community or a campus has an obligation to report accurately and fairly, to give space to what it opposes as much as to what it favors, to publish corrections where justified—and then to take any view it conscientiously wishes in its editorials, being sure to provide fair opportunity for rebuttal.

2. Mr. Barrett of the Commission considers the make-up of a publications board "of central importance." Repeatedly he has emphasized that "so long as a paper is financed largely out of student fees, such a board should represent students in serving as publisher of the paper. . . . Regular critiques of the paper by the board can be a major constructive force and should be accepted procedure."

It is submitted that there is need for all those concerned with the publication of a principal campus newspaper to think through what its role should be, to agree on a basic set of principles, and then to accord the editors as much freedom as possible within those principles.

The basic principles are not difficult. They include:

A clear distinction between news columns and editorial comment

Endeavoring conscentiously to give the readership a full and fair report of developments on the campus or affecting the campus

Faithful coverage of both sides—or, indeed, all sides—of any significant controversy

Competent coverage of important administration statements in the same sense that a responsible city daily reports the statements of mayor or the president

Confining opinion to the editorial page or to unmistakeably labeled opinion columns, but there being free to be as outspoken as desired

Readiness to correct mistakes with reasonable prominence in the paper

Affording ample opportunity for answers to editorial opinions

The worst shortcomings and offenses found among the newspapers on the various campuses, in the Commission's eyes, generally result from simple ineptitude and inexperience—sometimes from staff exhaustion.[3]

For these reasons the Commission recommends journalism seminars for staffs, stipends and other attractions sufficient to assure adequate manpower, and a paid adviser for each newspaper. It is not important for the adviser to be a member of faculty or administration; there are even arguments against this. What is important is for him to be an experienced professional, to know the institution, and to have the confidence of the staff. Sometimes a younger alumnus who has made his mark in journalism is the ideal for this position. He may serve either part time or full time but should be readily available during critical hours.[4]

3. Mr. Isaacs has taken particular exception to the practice of the California campus papers in publishing a standard disclaimer that "all other articles are the opinion of the individual writer." He holds this technique to be an abdication of editorial responsibility and one conducive to biased reporting and writing. He has argued that the practice in itself resulted in the publication of some of the most disputed articles during the 1968-69 year. He has stated, "To permit any volunteer entertainment reviewer laissez-faire freedom to write as he pleases, at whatever length he pleases, is to reduce editor and managing editor to figureheads and challenges the legitimacy of the editorial board role. An editor's judgment may be faulty in instances, but he is the administrator of the staff and it is his duty to pass the necessary judgments for a consistent news and editorial policy. Editors who refuse to accept such responsibility should be released and replaced."

4. Mr. Winship emphasizes the point that the adviser "must be wanted" by the staff and that "in no case should an adviser be forced upon the editorial board."

Number 4

The Commission recommends that the University of California, as a matter of policy, provide itself with alternative means of circulating official statements, interpretations, and news as appropriate on each campus. An official but modest university newsletter, issued infrequently except in time of particular need, can serve this purpose admirably.

There have been disagreements on some of the University of California campuses about the necessity of administrations' purchasing space in the student papers. The Commission agrees that campus newspapers should consider it a responsibility to publish important announcements. However, it is also aware that space limitations frequently are such that an official pronouncement printed in full would strip the newspaper of all other information. In such cases, the Commission considers paid space in a student newspaper a justified device for circulating official statements in full.

Official newsletters can go far toward overcoming occasional problems arising from differences over news judgments, space accorded official announcements, and administrators' unhappiness about student efforts to achieve journalistic "color" and "vigor" in reporting official actions.

The existence of such official journals, however, should not be used as reason or excuse for attempting to exclude student journalistic enterprise, or to discourage campus journalism, or to reduce funds presently allocated for this student activity. Nor should publication of such newsletters be so frequent or be so complete as to seem either to compete with student journals or to relieve them of their obligations to provide full, fair, and honest news reporting.

Number 5

The Commission has already noted that inadequate staffing and insufficient training are major obstacles to high quality performance in campus journalism at the University of California.

To these points, the Commission on July 11 made an interim recommendation to President Charles J. Hitch that the university consider sponsoring a professional seminar for student editors in early fall. The suggestion grew out of conferences with the student editors. When questioned directly later, they endorsed the proposal with enthusiasm.

It is the Commission's view that student editors need and welcome professional counsel. The type of seminars recommended call for the bringing in of skilled newspaper experts to offer counsel on the techniques of sound reporting, feature writing, constructive editing, proper typographical display, and other facets of normal professional performance.

Such seminars entail some university responsibility for funding. The Commission views this type of activity as part of the overall function of the university system, even though related to a voluntary campus activity.

Number 6

In connection with the above recommendation, the Commission is acutely conscious of the dichotomy inherent in its belief that, while campus newspapers should be operated independently, they also often require skilled counsel.

This is most evident where there are departments of journalism on campuses. On the one hand, the Commission believes these departments should not attempt to be informal guardians over the staffs; nor should they consider the campus newspapers as possible laboratory models. On the other hand, the Commission holds that these departments should be immediately ready to provide practical advice whenever such counsel is solicited by publications boards, editors, or staff members.

The problem of faculty counsel is more difficult on campuses where there are no instructors trained in journalistic methods and no professionals available. Several of the University of California campus editors told the Commission they had experienced frustration in their efforts to obtain mature guidance.

The Commission's recommendation is that in such cases the campus staffs seek out faculty representatives of their own choosing—and that the university administrators lend their support to such collaboration in providing invited advisers adequate time to provide the counsel sought by the student staffs.

To the Commission, the key to this problem rests on a basic understanding and acceptance of the basic issue. To student editors everywhere, advice is warmly welcome. Control is resisted. Where student staffs seek guidance, it should be offered readily and willingly.

Number 7

The Commission was asked specifically to direct itself to the issue of obscenities in the campus press. It has.

There are at least three approaches to the problem:

1. Ban certain words from the campus press. The Commission rejects

this as patently absurd. There is no limit to the number of words which some individuals can deem offensive.

2. Ignore the problem and hope that it will go away. Some members of the Commission come close to accepting this approach.

3. Call special seminars of student editors, professional newsmen, and educators and have the ramifications of the language issue explored calmly. The Commission would not favor special seminars on this subject but considers it logical that the matter would arise in the seminars proposed in recommendation 5.[5]

The Commission does not consider the problem of offensive language as it has existed in the University of California's student newspapers the major issue. Detailed examination of more than 150 separate issues of the various newspapers disclosed only sporadic use of language difficult for the older generation to accept. News and editorial matter for the most part was free of such strong terms.

The language issue centered on certain entertainment coverage. To this some regents and parents had expressed shocked protest. Some of the Commission members also raised eyebrows at a few cases of what seemed vulgarity for vulgarity's sake.

The theory advanced by editors and publications boards was that more freedom was allowed reviewers on the basis that the audience, being made up of students, was not "captive" as they considered the general public to be in purchasing a professional, commercial newspaper of general circulation. It is a theory rejected by the Commission as specious. They hold that editing standards should be uniform.

The Commission has agreed that there is little point in its dwelling nervously over how to control the use of foul language in campus newspapers. The Commission agreed further that the occasional use of such language represents a relatively minor issue compared to the immense

5. Mr. Winship has added, "Of the three possible courses of action, I prefer #2—to ignore the use of such language. This does not mean that I condone obscenities in print, but that I believe ignoring them will prove to be the quickest way to limit their use. Far from condoning obscene words, I deplore them, largely because they are a bore. Their shock value has largely disappeared through overuse, so they have become primarily a lazy, inexpressive and inexact way of writing, which is not up to students' high potential of self-expression. The use of obscenities has been exaggerated recently, but it seems to have passed its peak and is now waning. Why revive the issue by calling attention to it? Holding seminars would mainly serve to do just this. Finally, the issue of the forced use of dirty words is insignificant compared to the many other great unsolved issues facing society. I believe that either outlawing it or calling seminars about it will only give the problem far more status than it deserves. I join with the rest in wishing that the problem would go away, but I believe it is well on the way towards dying of natural causes. Let's save our energies for bigger battles."

unsolved social and economic problems about which most thoughtful individuals are concerned. To center on the obscenity issue is an exercise in futility and drains energy that should be directed to major issues.

Indeed, the Commission members were more concerned with instances of biased reporting and writing. Gutter language merely displays slovenly manners. Biased journalism distorts issues and misinforms.

Furthermore, the Commission is led to believe that the obscenity fad is waning among student editors and that the intelligently edited publications are recognizing that educated society can express itself with greater precision and clarity and taste than is possible with the language of the battlefield or back alley.

The Commission unanimously and vigorously agreed that no discussion of the obscenity issue could be complete without condemnation of the adult generation's examples to youth.

Many parents who object strenuously to material published in campus newspapers see nothing amiss in themselves purchasing with delight the latest in books advertised as containing the most sordid of language and conduct or in openly seeking tickets to the latest theater productions abounding in depiction of copulation.[6]

In some of the major California cities, "topless" and "bottomless" signs abound, advertising business establishments catering to the adult population. The Commission also cannot help but note that the state is the center of the motion picture industry, which countenances the grinding out of countless tawdry sex reels for so-called adult consumption. There are the business groups which issue occasional publications obviously catering to prurience.

These, and other, accepted adult tolerances are perhaps not within the Commission's purview. They are cited, however, because all the members of the Commission are agreed that they constitute a double standard which today's university student has every right to regard as proof of the mature

6. Mr. Barrett's comment: "As for the 'obscenity' issue, my advice is to relax and leave it to what the Supreme Court has called the prevailing standards of the community—in this case the student community. In the first place, it is inconsistent for adults to be too appalled at four-letter words while flocking to books and plays that are chock-full of them. In the second place, norms are changing on campus as on the Supreme Court bench. In the third place, campus papers are not destined for either nine-year-olds or for Aunt Minnies. Finally, student bodies will ultimately set the standards for the community and its press, and there is reason to believe that students are coming to discriminate between the vulgarism that serves a real purpose and that which is wanton, to question whether the most educated need adopt the imprecise and hackneyed language of the least educated. It has been said that the American public is often unwise in the short run but makes great sense over the long run. I am confident that, in spite of momentary fads and vogues, the same can be said of student opinion."

generation's hypocrisy. Until California's public officials, parents, and business executives express the same degrees of indignation over these practices, their protestations about campus journalism's laxity will deserve scant attention.

Number 8

The Commission has been deeply troubled by the evidences of a lack of trust on all sides. There has been open hostility shown by some of the student newspaper staffs toward the regents and administrators and a countervailing disgust on the part of regents for the campus newspapers.

To the Commission, it seems clear that student fees now apportioned to the campus newspapers cannot be cut off peremptorily. The hearings conducted made it obvious that none of the parties would be content with the result—students, faculties, administrators, or regents.

As already noted, only three of the present papers would stand any chance of survival, and these immediately in curtailed form. The others would disappear. Campus bulletin boards, informational kiosks, administration newsletters, or throw-away announcements could hardly be expected to fill the campus needs. The likelihood—conceded by almost every one of the administrative staffs—is that there would be introduced underground publications specializing in gossip, lurid articles, and character assassination.

The Commission overall is recommending a course of patience and understanding; of offering student editors counsel and training; of opening doors, rather than closing them, and, on the part of student staffs, of a search for fiscal responsibility as well as news and editorial responsibility; of a welcoming of publication board responsibility, thus protecting student newspapers from precensorship; and of a genuine search for the skills and good faith that lead to sound reporting, which is the underpinning of all courageous editorial commentary.

With good faith on all sides, the acidulous atmosphere of the past period should disappear. Men of good will can disagree strongly and vigorously without imputing evil motive to each other.

Given such good faith and good will, student journalists can sharpen the skills which later in professional life can lead to further advancement of the causes which impel all men of decent instinct.

Epilogue

The Commission prefaced this report with a brief quotation from the 1947 report of the Commission on Freedom of the Press. It was an inquiry financed by grants from Time, Inc., and Encyclopedia Britannica, Inc.

We have elected to close the report with the slightly longer conclusion of that distinguished group of scholars, which consisted of Dr. Robert M. Hutchins, then Chancellor of the University of Chicago; Professors Zechariah Chaffee, Jr., of Harvard; John M. Clark, Columbia; William E. Hocking, Harvard; Harold D. Lasswell, Yale; Charles E. Merriam, Chicago; Reinhold Niebuhr, Union Theological Seminary; Robert Redfield, Chicago; Arthur M. Schlesinger, Sr., Harvard; George N. Shuster, then President of Hunter College; Archibald MacLeish, former Assistant Secretary of State; and Beardsley Ruml, then Chairman of the New York Federal Reserve Bank. Their conclusion strikes us as equally applicable to America's student newspapers as to the American press generally.

The Enduring Goal and the Variable Realization

A free press is not a passing goal of human society; it is a necessary goal. For the press, taken in sum, is the swift self-expression of the experience of each moment of history; and this expression ought to be true. Much of the content of the press is intended solely for its own day; and the journalist sometimes reflects that his art is one of improvisation, and that its products, being destined to pass with the interest of the moment, require no great care in their workmanship. Yet, just because it is the day's report of itself, it is the permanent word of that day to all other days. The press must be free because its freedom is a condition of its veracity, and its veracity is its good faith with the total record of the human spirit.

At the same time, freedom of the press is certainly not an isolated value, nor can it mean the same in every society and at all times. It is a function within a society and must vary with the social context. It will be different in times of general security and in times of crisis; it will be different under varying states of public emotion and belief.

The freedom we have been examining has assumed a type of public mentality which may seem to us standard and universal, but which is, in many respects, a product of our special history—a mentality accustomed to the noise and confusion of clashing opinions and reasonably stable in temper when the fortunes of ideas are swiftly altered. But what a mind does with a fact or an opinion is widely different when that mind is serene and when it is anxious; when it has confidence in its environment and when it is infected with suspicion or resentment; when it is gullible and when it is well furnished with the means of criticism; when it has hope and when it is in despair.

Further, the consumer is a different man when he has to judge his press alone and when his judgment is steadied by other social agencies. Free and diverse utterance may result in bewilderment unless he has access—through home, church, school, custom—to interpreting patterns of thought and feeling. There is no such thing as press "objectivity" unless the mind of the reader can identify the objects dealt with.

Whether at any time and place the psychological conditions exist under which a free press has social significance is always a question of fact, not of theory. These mental conditions may be lost. They may also be created. The press itself is always one of the chief agents in destroying or in building the bases of its own significance.

Respectfully submitted
by the Special Commission

NORMAN E. ISAACS, Chairman

WILLIAM B. ARTHUR

EDWARD W. BARRETT

THOMAS WINSHIP